Access™ for Windows™ Quick Reference

Que Quick Reference Series

Lisa Monitto

Access for Windows Quick Reference

Copyright © 1993 by Que® Corporation

All rights reserved. Printed in the United States of America. No part of this book may be used or reproduced in any form or by any means, or stored in a database or retrieval system, without prior written permission of the publisher except in the case of brief quotations embodied in critical articles and reviews. Making copies of any part of this book for any purpose other than your own personal use is a violation of United States copyright laws. For information, address Que Corporation, 11711 N. College Ave., Carmel, IN 46032.

Library of Congress Catalog No.: 93-83867

ISBN: 1-56529-233-2

This book is sold *as is*, without warranty of any kind, either express or implied, respecting the contents of this book, including but not limited to implied warranties for the book's quality, performance, merchantability, or fitness for any particular purpose. Neither Que Corporation nor its dealers or distributors shall be liable to the purchaser or any other person or entity with respect to any liability, loss, or damage caused or alleged to have been caused directly or indirectly by this book.

96 95 94 93   4 3 2 1

Interpretation of the printing code: the rightmost double-digit number is the year of the book's printing; the rightmost single-digit number, the number of the book's printing. For example, a printing code of 93-1 shows that the first printing of the book occurred in 1993.

Screen reproductions in this book were created with Collage Plus from Inner Media, Inc., Hollis, NH.

All terms mentioned in this book that are known to be trademarks or service marks have been appropriately capitalized. Que cannot attest to the accuracy of this information. Use of a term in this book should not be regarded as affecting the validity of any trademark or service mark.

Publisher
David P. Ewing

Associate Publisher
Rick Ranucci

Title Manager
Walter R. Bruce III

Acquisitions Editor
Sarah Browning

Production Editor
Colleen Totz

Editors
Tracy L. Barr
William A. Barton

Technical Editor
Michael Gilbert

Book Designer
Amy Peppler-Adams

Production Team
Julie Brown, Laurie Casey, Heather Kaufman,
Bob LaRoche, Joy Dean Lee, Caroline Roop

Table of Contents

Introduction 1
What Is Microsoft Access? 1
Using This Book 2
Conventions Used in This Book......3

1 Microsoft Access Basics 5
Installing Microsoft Access 5
Getting Started 6
The Microsoft Access Screen.........7
Help 9
Cue Cards 10
Windows 11
Customizing Access 12
Keyboard Shortcuts 26

2 Databases 33
Creating a Database 33
Opening a Database 34
Modifying a Database 35
Encrypting and Decrypting 36
Repairing a Database 38
Closing a Database 38
Exiting Access 39

3 Tables 41
Creating Tables 41
Creating Fields 42
Using Keys 43
Saving Tables 44
Copying Tables 44
Switching Views 45
Properties 46
Relationships 47
Closing Table Design or Datasheet View 48

4 Attaching, Importing, and Exporting Tables — 49
Attaching Tables 49
Importing Data 50
Exporting Data 55

5 Working with Datasheets — 61
Datasheets 61
Viewing Datasheet Records 62
Adding a New Record 63
Moving between Records 64
Multiuser Data Entry 65
The Clipboard 66
Removing Data 67
Appending Records 68
Undo 69
Objects and OLE 69
Embedding Objects 71
Linking Objects 72
Selecting Records 73
Saving Changes To a Record 74
Searching 74
Row Height 77
Column Width 78
Hidden Columns 78
Frozen Columns 79
Fonts 80
Gridlines 81
Closing a Datasheet 81
Saving a Datasheet 81
Design View 82
Printing 82

6 Query by Example — 87
Creating a Query 87
Select Queries 87
Running a Query 88
Saving a Query in Design View 89
Saving a Query in Datasheet View 90
Changing the Name 91

Closing the Design Window............................91
Criteria 92
Operators 92
Calculations 94
Grouping Data 97
Adding and Deleting Rows 98
Adding and Removing Tables 99
Joins 100
Append Queries 102
Crosstab Queries 104
Delete Queries 106
Make Table Queries 107
Update Queries 108
Parameter Queries 109
Properties 110
SQL 113
Controlling the Display 113
Saving Changes 114
Listing Queries 114
Printing a Query 115

7 Forms 119
Creating Forms 119
Using FormWizards 120
Opening Forms 122
Form View 122
Datasheet View 123
Design View 124
Subform 125
Palette Window 125
Ruler 126
Toolbox 126
Selecting Controls 127
Tab Order of Controls 127
Aligning Controls 128
Bring to Front, Send to Back 130
The Form Design Grid 130
Sizing Controls 131
Properties 131
Headers and Footers 133
Filters 134
Saving Forms 135

Printing 136
Closing the Form Design Window 140

8 Reports 141
Creating a Report 141
Using the ReportWizard 142
Opening Reports...144
Sorting and Grouping 145
Calculated Controls.......................................146
Headers and Footers 147
Printing 148
Saving Reports 152
Changing Names 153
Closing the Report Design Window 153

9 Macros 155
Creating Macros 155
Opening an Existing Macro 156
Running a Macro...157
Displaying Columns.......................................159
Changing the Name 160
Saving the Macro 161
Closing the Macro Design Window 161

10 Security 163
User Accounts...163
Modifying Passwords 165
Groups 166
Permissions 167

11 Access Basic 169
Creating Access Basic Modules 169
Opening an Existing Module 170
Importing Code 170
Saving Modules 171
Setting and Clearing Breakpoints 172
Debugging..173
Displaying Modules and Procedures 176

Index 179

Introduction

Welcome to *Access for Windows Quick Reference*. This book is designed as a handy guide and reference for both new and experienced users of Microsoft's Access for Windows database management software. The book assumes a familiarity with Microsoft Windows, but does not assume that you have ever used Access.

What Is Microsoft Access?

Microsoft Access for Windows is a full-featured *relational database management system* (RDBMS) designed to run in Microsoft Windows. Access uses the graphical power of Windows to the utmost so that you can easily view and work with your data in an intuitive fashion, giving you visual access to your data.

Access makes your data available to you quickly and easily, and presents it in an effective and readable way. Its powerful *Query by Example* (QBE) capabilities help you to locate the information you need with just a few keystrokes.

Microsoft Access allows you to look at your data in a variety of ways. Sometimes the information in a record is easier to understand if the record's fields are arranged on a form or a report in a visually pleasing way; sometimes you need to see the maximum number of data records possible on your screen.

A Microsoft Access form is a special window that is used for data entry. You can use the visual power of Windows to create an attractive form using a combination of graphics and text. Microsoft Access forms can present your data in a format that is easier to read and understand than a datasheet.

Also provided with Microsoft Access are FormWizards, special tools that help you create data-entry forms by asking you to answer some basic questions about how you want to present your data and then doing the layout work for you.

Access makes it easy for you to create attractive printed reports based on multiple tables or queries. ReportWizards are special tools provided with Microsoft Access that help you create reports by asking you to answer some basic questions about how you want to present your data and then doing all the layout work for you. The Report Design view enables you to start a report from scratch or customize a report that ReportWizard helped you design.

In Microsoft Access, you can create and edit sophisticated databases and maintain them without knowing a programming language. Access Basic provides a programmer with additional abilities to automate and extend the functionality of a database.

In addition to Access Basic, macros add to the capabilities of your database. A macro is a sequence of built-in commands, or *actions* that you put together that Microsoft Access can carry out.

Another important feature that Microsoft Access offers is system security. Authorized users and guests are forced to log on to Microsoft Access by entering a user name and password in the Logon dialog box.

Using This Book

Access for Windows Quick Reference includes eleven chapters, organized by the way you use Access. The chapters range from Chapter 1, "Microsoft Access

Basics," to Chapter 11, "Access Basic." When you are working in Access and get stuck, or simply want some guidance before you get started, use the Table of Contents to find the appropriate section. Alternatively, you can use the Index at the back of the book to assist you in locating the information you need.

Each chapter in the book is organized by task. Similar or related tasks are grouped together to make it easier for you to quickly find all the help you need.

This quick reference covers all of the most often performed tasks in Access in a quick and concise manner. Whenever you feel that you are in need of a more detailed discussion, turn to *Using Access for Windows,* Special Edition, also from Que, for the best and most complete coverage of Microsoft Access available.

Conventions Used in This Book

To make the information as clear to you as possible, this book follows certain conventions. For example, when a keyboard key has a special name, such as F1 or Del, the name appears exactly that way in the test. When you are instructed to choose a menu command, the shortcut key is boldfaced (**F**ile, for example).

When you must select a series of menu selections to initiate a command, they are listed in the order that you select them. For example, **F**ile **S**ave means that you first select **F**ile and then choose **S**ave.

For easy reference, this book contains special text boxes for shortcut methods to perform the operations discussed in a section. When appropriate, a corresponding tool bar button also appears in the box.

Microsoft Access Basics

Microsoft Access is a *relational database management system* (RDBMS) for the Microsoft Windows operating environment. Access uses the graphical power of Windows to the utmost so that you can easily view and work with your data in an intuitive fashion, giving you visual access to your data.

Access makes your data available to you quickly and easily, and presents it in an effective and readable way. Its powerful *Query by Example* (QBE) capabilities help you to locate the information you need with just a few keystrokes.

Installing Microsoft Access

Installing Access is simple. Insert the first disk into a floppy drive, choose Run from the File Manager File menu, and type **a:setup** (or **b:setup**, depending on which drive you are using). The setup program asks you to specify a directory in which to install Microsoft Access. The default directory is C:\ACCESS. If you want to install Access in a different directory, enter a valid directory path name in the **Install in:** text box. If you enter the name of a directory that does not exist, Setup creates a directory for you.

6 ACCESS FOR WINDOWS QUICK REFERENCE

Setup then checks your hard drive for existing copies of Microsoft Access and checks to see whether you have enough space available for the program on your hard drive.

Access has three installation options: Complete, Custom, and Minimum. Choose the option you want. Setup begins installation and prompts you for the disks it needs to proceed.

If you have enough disk space, you should choose Complete Installation. Choosing this option ensures that all the parts of the program will be installed on your hard drive in their proper directories. After you have used Access and familiarized yourself with some of its features, you can delete the sample databases and auxiliary files if you need the extra disk space that these items take up.

Getting Started

Setup creates a Microsoft Access group in your Program Manager. Click on the Microsoft Access icon in this group to start the program.

When you run Access for the first time, the first thing you see is the Welcome to Microsoft Access dialog box, as shown in figure 1.1.

There are three small buttons beside the descriptions in the dialog box: Create a New Database, Explore a Sample Database, and Get a Quick Introduction. If you are new to databases and to Microsoft Access, select Get a Quick Introduction for a quick tour of what Access can do.

After you sample all three of the buttons on the Welcome to Microsoft Access dialog box, you can select the check box in the lower left corner. If you leave it unchecked, this welcome screen appears each time you start Access. After you select this check box and exit Access, this dialog box no longer appears each time you start the program.

MICROSOFT ACCESS BASICS **7**

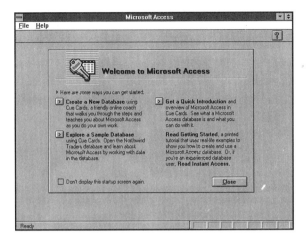

Figure 1.1. The Welcome to Microsoft Access dialog box.

The Microsoft Access Screen

The Microsoft Access screen is the background for all Microsoft Access operations. On this screen you will find the basic elements of a Microsoft Windows program (see fig. 1.2).

When you create or open a database, the Database window appears. The Database window is the main window in Microsoft Access. From this window you can open any object in your database. For more information on the Database window, see Chapter 2, "Databases."

The Microsoft Access screen and the Database window are made up of the following parts:

- *Title Bar.* The title bar is the colored bar at the top of the screen. It normally contains the program's name, the Control Menu box, and the Minimize, Maximize, and Restore buttons.

8 ACCESS FOR WINDOWS QUICK REFERENCE

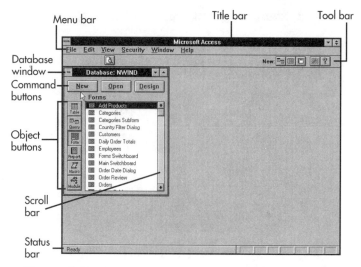

Figure 1.2. The Microsoft Access screen.

- *Scroll bars.* The scroll bars are rectangular regions at the right and bottom edges of a screen, a window, or a list box. Their presence on a window or list box indicates that more data is present than can be viewed at one time in the window or list box. With scroll bars, you can use a mouse to move quickly through your data.

- *Menu bar.* The menu bar gives you access to commands and additional cascading menus that you can use to create and modify objects in your database. In Microsoft Access, each type of window has its own menu bar that has different commands available, depending on the current selected object. (The menu commands can change when you edit different database objects.)

- *Tool bar.* The tool bar is located beneath the menu bar. It contains small buttons that perform common operations when you click on them. The tool bar buttons can be thought of as a menu shortcut, since they frequently represent actions that otherwise must be accessed through several layers of cascading menus. Like the menu bar, the tool bar buttons available to you will differ, depending on which database object you are currently editing.

- *Database window.* The Database window provides you with an overview of the different objects that your database contains. Clicking on one of the object buttons on the left side of the Database window shows you the list of names for each type of object that your database contains. The Database window offers several ways of creating, viewing, and editing your data.

- *Object buttons.* The Object buttons on the side represent all the types of objects your database can contain. A Microsoft Access database can contain tables, queries, forms, macros, and modules. Clicking on an object button gives you direct access to run, inspect, or modify all the objects of that object type.

- *Command buttons.* The three command buttons at the top of the database window allow you to create a new database object, open an object for data entry, or open an object for design modifications.

- *Status bar.* The Status bar (at the bottom of the screen) displays informative messages about the mode of the current window on the left side and status of the locking keys such as Caps Lock, Num Lock, Scroll Lock, or Insert on the right side.

Help

Microsoft Access provides context-sensitive assistance through its Help menu. Use Help when you need information about a database object. The Help menu is available from every window in Microsoft Access.

To open the Table of Contents
To see a list of general help topics, choose **Help** Contents.

> **Shortcuts:** Press the F1 key.
>
> Click on the Help tool bar button.

To search for help on a specific term

To search Microsoft Access Help for help on a specific term or process:

1 Choose **H**elp **S**earch. The Search dialog box appears.

2 Enter the term for which you want help in the text box, or select a term from the list.

3 Choose the **S**how Topics button to see a list of subtopics concerning the help term you have selected.

4 Select a help subtopic from the list and then choose the **G**oto button.

5 To exit Help, choose **F**ile E**x**it to return to Microsoft Access.

Cue Cards

Cue Cards are step-by-step instructions that show you how to use many of the commands in Microsoft Access. Unlike most tutorials, which teach you how to use a program's commands by letting you practice on sample data, Microsoft Access Cue Cards are displayed on-screen next to the database that you want to work on. Cue Cards help you learn Microsoft Access commands while you get your own work done.

To open the Cue Card menu

To open the Cue Card main menu, choose **H**elp **C**ue Cards.

Windows

All data entry and editing of database objects in Microsoft Access is done in windows. When more than one window is open, the commands described in the following sections can help you size and arrange them.

To arrange minimized icons

When several windows are open in Microsoft Access, you may opt to minimize one or more of them so that more room is available on-screen. To arrange all icons of all the minimized windows in a row across the bottom of the Microsoft Access window, choose **W**indow **A**rrange Icons.

To cascade windows

To arrange all open non-minimized windows in Microsoft Access in an overlapping manner so that the title bar of each window is displayed, choose **W**indow **C**ascade.

To tile windows

To arrange all open non-minimized windows in Microsoft Access side-by-side so that all windows are displayed and don't overlap, choose **W**indow **T**ile.

To hide a window

To hide the active window from view, choose **W**indow **H**ide.

To redisplay a hidden window

To redisplay windows that have been removed from sight with the Window Hide command:

1 Choose **W**indow **S**how. The Show Window dialog box appears.

2 Select a name from the list of hidden windows in the **W**indow list.

3 Click on the OK button.

When there are no hidden windows, this command is disabled or *grayed out* on the menu.

If all open windows are hidden, this command appears on the File menu in the Microsoft Access window.

To switch to an open window

Microsoft Access allows you to open up to nine windows at one time. To see a list of all open windows, or make active a window that is overlapped or minimized, select Window 1, 2, 3...9.

When you select an open window, you make that document active. A check mark appears in front of the name of the active window.

Customizing Access

Access enables you to customize the way the program looks and operates. You can set global defaults for many values.

To change environment preferences

To examine or edit your preferences for the way Microsoft Access looks and behaves:

1 Choose **View Options**. The Options dialog box appears.

2 Choose the category of the preference you want to view or change by scrolling through the **Category** list.

   The list of options for each category appears in the Items list.

3 Select an item. When standard options are available for you to choose from, an arrow appears next to the item text box. Sometimes you must enter a value in the text box with the keyboard.

General options

Option	Possible Values	Effect
Show Status Bar	Yes/No	Select Yes to display the status bar at the bottom of the screen; select No to hide it.
Show System Objects	Yes/No	Select Yes if you want to see the system objects displayed in the Database Window with your own database objects; select No to hide them from view.
OLE/DDE Timeout	From 0 to 300	Enter the number of seconds for Microsoft Access to continue trying to complete an OLE or DDE operation.
Show tool bar	Yes/No	Select Yes to show the beneath the Menu bar; select No to hide it from view.
Confirm Document Deletions	Yes/No	Select Yes if you want Microsoft Access to confirm the deletion of a database object; select No to set delete confirmation off.

continues

Option	Possible Values	Effect
Confirm Action Queries	Yes/No	Select Yes if you want Microsoft Access to confirm if you want to run an action query that might change data; select No to set action query confirmation off.
New Database Sort Order	General / Traditional/ Spanish/ Dutch/ Nordic	Select the sort order that best matches the character set that your data will be entered in.
Ignore DDE Requests	Yes/No	Select Yes to ignore requests for DDE (Dynamic Data Exchange) from all other applications; select No if you want Microsoft Access to respond to DDE requests.
Default Find/ Replace Behavior	Fast Search/ General Search	Select Fast Search if you want Microsoft Access to search the current field and

MICROSOFT ACCESS BASICS

Option	Possible Values	Effect
		match the whole field as its default Find/Replace search method.
		Select General Search if you want the default search method to check all fields and find a match within part of any field.
Default Database Directory	A valid existing path name	Enter the name of the directory that you want Microsoft Access to use as the default directory for database files.
Confirm Record Changes	Yes/No	Select Yes if you want Microsoft Access to confirm any record changes or deletions before making them permanent; select No to set record change confirmation off.

Keyboard options

Option	Possible Values	Effect
Arrow Key Behavior	Next Field/ Next Character	Select Next Field if you want to use the arrow keys to change focus from one field to another; select Next Character if you want to use the arrow keys to move the cursor within a field.
Move After Enter	No/ Next Field/ Next Record	Select No if you don't want the Enter key to change the focus of a field or control; select Next field if you want the Enter key to change the focus to the next control or field in the tab order. Select Next Record if you want the Enter key to change the focus to the first field of the next record.
Cursor Stops at First/Last Field	Yes/No	Select Yes if you want Microsoft Access to prevent the cursor from changing to another row when you use the

Option	Possible Values	Effect
		left- and right-arrow keys to move through the fields in a row; select No if you want the cursor to move to the next row when you press the right-arrow key in the last field of a row, or move to the previous row if you press the left-arrow key in the first field of a row.
Key Assignment Macro	The name of a macro in the current database	If you want to change the name of the macro that Microsoft Access uses to make macro/key assignments, enter the name of a macro.

Printing options

Option	Possible Values	Effect
Left Margin	0 to width of page	Enter a value to change the default left margin of a datasheet, module, form, or report.

continues

Option	Possible Values	Effect
Right Margin	0 to width of page	Enter a value to change the default right margin of a datasheet, module, form, or report.
Top Margin	0 to height of page	Enter a value to change the default top margin of a datasheet, module, form, or report.
Bottom Margin	0 to height of page	Enter a value to change the default bottom margin of a datasheet, module, form, or report.

Form & Report Design options

Option	Possible Values	Effect
Form Template	Name of a form in the current database	Enter the name of the form that you want Microsoft when Access to use as the default when you create a new form with the FormWizard.

MICROSOFT ACCESS BASICS

Option	Possible Values	Effect
Report Template	Name of a report in the current database	Enter the name of the report you want Microsoft Access to use as the default when you create a new report with the ReportWizard.
Objects Snap To Grid	Yes/No	Select Yes if you want new controls on a form to automatically align to the grid when you place them; select No if you do not want new controls to automatically align.
Show Grid	Yes/No	Select Yes to have a new form or report display a grid; select No to hide the grid in new forms and reports.
Selection Behavior	Partially Enclosed/ Fully Enclosed	Select Partially Enclosed if you want the pointer to select controls on a form or a report if they are touched by the selection rectangle; select

continues

Option	Possible Values	Effect
		No if you want to specify that controls must be completely enclosed by the selection rectangle to be selected.
Show Ruler	Yes/No	Select Yes to see rulers at the top and left side of the Form Design or Report Design windows; select No to hide the rulers from view.

Datasheet options

Option	Possible Values	Effect
Default Gridlines Behavior	On/Off	Select On to view a datasheet's gridlines; select Off to hide them from view.
Default Column Width	From 0 to 22 inches or from 0 to 55.87 cm	Enter a value in inches, centimeters, or twips that you want Microsoft Access to use for the default column width.

Option	Possible Values	Effect
Default Font Name	Name of an installed font	Enter the name of the font that you want Microsoft Access to use as the default for all new datasheets.
Default Font size	Valid size for the default font	Enter the size of the default font that will be used to display a datasheet's data and field names.
Default Font Weight	Thin/ Extra Light/ Normal/ Medium/ Semi-Bold/ Bold/ Extra Bold/ Heavy	Select the weight of the default font.
Default Font Italic	Yes/No	Select Yes to display the data and field names of new datasheets in italic. Select No to turn italic off.
Default Font Underline	Yes/No	Select Yes to display the data and field names of new datasheets underlined. Select No to turn underlining off.

Query Design options

Option	Possible Values	Effect
Restrict Available Fields	Yes/No	Select Yes if you want to see only fields from the QBE grid in the query's field list; select No to see all fields in all the underlying tables.
Run With Owner's Permissions	Yes/No	Select Yes if you want users who are restricted from looking at a query's underlying tables to be able to look at the data resulting from a new query; select No to prevent users from seeing the data in a new query.
Show Table Names	Yes/No	Select Yes to display table names in the QBE grid in new queries; select No to hide them from view.

Macro Design options

Option	Possible Values	Effect
Show Macro Names Column	Yes/No	Select Yes to display the Macro Name Name column by default in new macros; select No to hide the Macro Name column by default.
Show Conditions Column	Yes/No	Select Yes to display the Conditions column by default in new macros; select No to hide the Conditions column by default.

Module Design options

Option	Possible Values	Effect
Syntax Checking	Yes/No	Select Yes if you want Access Basic to check for the correct syntax when you enter each line of code; select No if you want to disable syntax checking.

continues

ACCESS FOR WINDOWS QUICK REFERENCE

Option	Possible Values	Effect
Tab Stop Width	From 1 to 30	Enter the number of spaces that you want to use for tab stops in the Module window.

Multiuser options

Option	Possible Values	Effect
Default Record Locking	No Locks/ All Records/ Edited Records	Select No Locks to disable all record locking; select All Records to lock all the records in any open database object so that other users are prevented from accessing them; select Edited Records to lock only the current record in an open table, query, or form.
Default Open Mode for Databases	Exclusive/ Shared	Select Exclusive to prevent more than one user from opening a database at one time; select

Option	Possible Values	Effect
		Shared to allow a database to be opened by more than one user more at a time.
Refresh Interval	From 1 to 32,766	Enter the number of seconds that you want Microsoft Access to wait before updating records in a shared form or datasheet.
Update Retry	From 0 to 1,000	Enter the number of milliseconds you want Microsoft Access to retry saving a record that is locked by another user.
Number of Update Retries	From 0 to 10	Enter the number of attempts Microsoft Access should make to save a record that is locked by another user.

continues

Option	Possible Values	Effect
ODBC Refresh Interval	From 1 to 3600	Enter the time in seconds for Microsoft Access to wait before updating records that you are editing using ODBC.

The View Options menu selection is available from every menu except the Startup menu.

Keyboard Shortcuts

Almost all of the commands in Microsoft Access are accessible by mouse or keyboard. You may use either, depending on whether you are more comfortable using the mouse or the keyboard.

The function keys are listed below in four sets: keys used throughout Microsoft Access, keys used in the Design view, keys used in the Datasheet view and Form view, and keys used in the Module window.

Global keys that have the same function from all screens in Microsoft Access

Key	Function
F1	Starts Microsoft Access Help. If you press F1 while a command, dialog box, property, control, action, or Access Basic keyword is selected, Microsoft Access Help displays context-sensitive information about the currently selected command or object.

Key	Function
Shift+F1	Displays a question mark pointer. You can then move the pointer to any part of the current screen or windows and select an item. Microsoft Access Help displays context-sensitive information about what you select.
Ctrl+F4	Closes the current window without exiting Microsoft Access.
Alt+F4	When selected from a dialog box, Alt+F4 closes the dialog box. Otherwise, Alt+F4 closes all open windows and exits Microsoft Access. Microsoft Access prompts you to save any unsaved data.
Ctrl+F6	If more than one window is open, Ctrl+F6 cycles through them, making successive windows current and bringing them to the front of any overlapping windows.
F11 or Alt+F1	Makes the Database window visible and current if it is hidden behind other windows, or minimized.
F12 or Alt+F2	Permits you to save a new database, or make a copy of the current database and save it under a new name.
Shift+F12 or Alt+Shift+F2	Saves any modifications in the current database object.

Keys used in Design view

Key	Function
F2	Toggles from Editing mode to Navigation mode in the Design view of tables, queries, and macros. If you press the F2 key on a selected field, Microsoft Access allows you to enter information in that field, and the arrow keys move the cursor only within the field. Pressing F2 again ends editing mode, and the arrow keys change the focus to the prior or next field.
Shift+F2	Opens the Zoom dialog box. The Zoom dialog box makes it easier to see and enter data in small fields that are not easily visible.
F6	In the Design view of tables and queries, or in the filter design, the window is divided into a top and bottom section. F6 toggles the active section of the window.

Keys used in Datasheet view and Form view

Key	Function
F2	Toggles from Edit mode to Navigation mode in the Design view of tables, queries, and macros. Pressing F2 when the cursor is on a field allows you to enter information in that field, and the arrow keys move the cursor within the field. Pressing F2 again ends Editing

Key	Function
	mode, and the arrow keys change the focus to the prior or next field.
F4	Expands the selected combo box or drop-down list box.
Shift+F4	Looks for the next occurrence of the last text that you searched for using the Find or Replace dialog box.
F5	Allows you to manually enter a record number to jump to in the record number box at the bottom of the table window.
F6	Toggles between the sections of a form in Form view. Pressing F6 moves the focus to the header, detail section, and footer of the form.
Shift+F6	Cycles through the sections of a form in Form View in reverse order. Pressing F6 moves the focus to the footer, detail section, and header of the form.
F7	Searches for specific text. Opens the Find dialog box.
Shift+F7	Searches for specific text and optionally replace it. Opens the Replace dialog box.
F8	Turns on Extended Select mode. You can extend your selection by pressing F8 multiple times. This extends your selection to the current word, the field containing the word, the record containing that field, and finally all records.

continues

Key	Function
Shift+F8	Deselects in reverse order of Extended Select mode. Narrow selection from all records, a single record, a field in that record, to the current word in that field. Press **Esc** to cancel Extend mode.
F9	Recalculates values for all the fields in the current window.
Shift+F9	Runs all active queries and update the tables they are based on.

Keys used in the Module window

Key	Function
F2	Displays a list box that shows all the procedures contained in the module.
Shift+F2	Displays the procedure selected in the Module window.
F3	Finds the next occurrence of the last text that you searched for using the Find or Replace dialog box.
Shift+F3	Finds the previous occurrence of the last text you searched for using the Find or Replace dialog box.
F5	Continues the execution of module code after a break or halt.
F6	Toggles between the upper and lower sections of the Module window.

Key	Function
F7	Searches for specific text. Opens the Find dialog box.
Shift+F7	Searches for specific text and optionally replaces it with new text or nothing. Opens the Replace dialog box.
F8	Executes the code in a module, one step at a time.
Shift+F8	Same as F8, but does not trace through procedure calls.
F9	Toggles a breakpoint that causes a break in execution of code on or off at the selected line in the module.

2

Databases

The term *database* has traditionally referred to a series of data records placed together in a file. Microsoft Access expands the definition of the word *database* to refer to all the parts of a database application.

In Microsoft Access, a database is a container for *data tables* (series of data records); forms for data entry; queries for selection of data, reports, and macros; and modules that perform special operations on the data and make entering new data easy. All these parts of the database are referred to individually as *database objects*.

Creating a Database

When you create a new database, you create a special file that holds your data tables, forms, queries, reports, macros, and modules.

To create a new database
To create a new database:

1 Choose File New Database. The New Database dialog box appears.

2 Enter the name of a database file in the File Name text box, or select a file from the file list and choose OK.

3 If the database file name you selected already exists, Microsoft Access asks whether you want to replace it. Respond appropriately.

The blank database window appears.

If you enter the name of a database that already exists as the name for your new database, Microsoft Access informs you that if you proceed the original database will be overwritten.

Opening a Database

Open an existing database when you want to look at or modify data or modify the structure of a database object.

To open a database

To open an existing database:

1 Choose File Open Database. The Open Database dialog box appears.

2 Enter the name of a database file in the File Name text box, or select a file from the file list and click on the OK button.

To open a database for read-only access, select the Read Only check box in the Open Database dialog box.

To open a database for your exclusive access, select the Exclusive check box in the Open Database dialog box.

The Database menu replaces the Startup menu after you open a database.

To access a recently used database

For quick access to the four database files you have opened most recently, select File **1** (2, 3, or 4).

Modifying a Database

When you add, modify, and delete data, the data in the database file may become fragmented and, consequently, store less efficiently. If this situation occurs, you can compact the database to solve the problem. In addition, when you design the database, you may need to change the name of a table, form, query, report, macro, or module. The commands discussed in the following sections modify the database file.

To compact a database

To eliminate fragmentation and wasted space in a database:

1 Choose **F**ile **C**ompact Database. The Database To Compact From dialog box appears.

2 Enter the name of the database file you want to compact in the File **N**ame text box, or select a database file from the file list and click on the OK button. The Database To Compact Into dialog box appears.

3 Enter a new database name in the File **N**ame text box, or select a database from the file list and then click on the OK button.

4 If a database file with the name you have entered already exists, Microsoft Access informs you that the file will be replaced and asks whether you want to continue compacting.

If you are using Microsoft Access on a network and another user has opened the file you want to compact, the command aborts.

To change the name of a database object

To change the name of a form, table, query, report, macro, or module in the current database:

1 From the list in the Database Window, select the database object you want to rename.

2 Choose **F**ile Rena**m**e. The Rename dialog box appears with the original object's name in the title bar.

3 Enter a new name for the object in the text box and click on the OK button.

If you change the name of a database object, any references in other database objects to the original name generate an error message because they refer to something that no longer exists.

To prevent errors from occurring, when you change the name of a database object, always search for and update any references to the object that use the original name so that Microsoft Access can locate it.

Encrypting and Decrypting

Microsoft Access normally stores data in an unencrypted form within a database file, which means that if the file is inspected with a file viewer, field names and data can be seen and read. To prevent others from seeing your data and field names, use the File Encrypt command. To make field names and data visible again, you use the File Decrypt command.

To encrypt a database
To make an encrypted copy of a database:

1 Choose **F**ile **E**ncrypt/Decrypt. The Encrypt/Decrypt dialog box appears.

2 Enter a database name in the File **N**ame text box, or choose the database you want encrypted from the file list. The Encrypt Database As dialog box appears.

3 In the File **N**ame text box, enter a name for the database file that you want to encrypt, or select the name of an existing database file from the file list and click on the OK button.

DATABASES **37**

If you enter a new name for the encrypted database file, the name can contain up to eight characters in any combination of letters and numbers, excluding spaces and punctuation characters.

If you enter the name of a file that already exists, Microsoft Access informs you that the file will be overwritten and asks whether you want to continue the operation.

To decrypt a database

To decrypt an encrypted database:

1 Choose File Encrypt/Decrypt. The Encrypt/Decrypt dialog box appears.

2 Enter a database name in the File Name text box or choose the database you want decrypted from the file list. The Decrypt Database As dialog box appears.

3 Enter a name for the database file that is being decrypted in the File Name text box, or select the name of an existing database file from the file list and click on the OK button.

If you enter a new name for the decrypted database file, the name can contain up to eight characters in any combination of letters and numbers, excluding spaces or punctuation characters.

If you enter the name of a file that already exists, Microsoft Access informs you that the file will be replaced and asks whether you want to continue the operation.

The Encrypt/Decrypt Database command works only on a database that is not currently open. If you are using Microsoft Access on a network and another user is working on the database you want to encrypt or decrypt, the other user must close the database before you can use this command.

Repairing a Database

If a database file becomes corrupted due to power loss during a write operation or a bad sector on the drive where the file is stored, you may be able to recover the file with the File Repair command.

To repair a database
To repair a corrupted database:

1 Choose **F**ile **R**epair Database. The Repair Database dialog box appears.

2 Enter the name of a database file in the File **N**ame text box, or select a file from the file list and click on the OK button.

Microsoft Access indicates whether the repair operation was successful.

Closing a Database

When you finish working with one database and want to open another, you must close the open database first.

To close a database
To close the current database, choose **F**ile **C**lose Database.

If you have not saved the changes you have made to the structure of your database, Microsoft Access prompts you to save your work.

> **Shortcut:** Press Ctrl+F4.

Exiting Access

When you finish working with a database, you exit Microsoft Access. Saving your work first is a good idea, but if you forget, Access asks you to save your modifications before exiting the program.

To end an Access session

To end your session with Microsoft Access, choose **F**ile E**x**it.

If you made any modifications to the structure or design of an existing database or if you created a new database, Microsoft Access prompts you to save your work.

> **Shortcut:** Press Alt+F4.

Tables

In Access, all data is stored in *tables*. Tables are made up of columns (known as *fields*) and rows (known as *records*). Each Access table is stored in an Access database. Before you can enter data into a table you must create the table.

This chapter decribes how to create a table, create fields in a table, assign key fields, copy tables, switch table views, set table properties, set table relationships, and close the design view of a table.

Creating Tables

A *table* is the database object that holds your data. Data is contained in a series of records that are further divided into fields of related information. When you create a table, you must specify a field for every item of data in a record and select the field type.

The Table menu appears whenever you open or switch to a table window. You can open a table in Design view or in Datasheet view.

To create a new table
To create a new table in the current database; Choose File New Table. The Table Window Design view appears.

> **Shortcut:** Click on the Table object button in the Database window, and then choose the New button by pressing Alt+N or clicking on the New button once.

To display the list of tables in the database
To view a list of all tables in a database in the Database window, choose **V**iew **T**ables. The list of tables appears in the Database window.

> **Shortcut:** Click on the Table object button on the left side of the Database window.

To open an existing table
To open a table in Datasheet view:

1 Select a table name from the list of tables in the Database window.

2 Choose the **O**pen command button by pressing Alt+O or clicking on the **O**pen button.

> **Shortcut:** Double-click on the table name you want to open in the Database window.

Creating Fields

Fields are part of the records in a database table. A *record* can consist of one or more fields of the same or varying data type. In Table Design view, a record is referred to as a *field row*.

To insert a field row
To create a new, blank field row above the selected field row in a table in Table Design view, choose **E**dit **I**nsert Row.

> **Shortcut:** Click on the field selector to the left of the field name and press the Insert key.

To delete field rows

To delete one or more selected field rows from a table in Table Design view:

1 Select one or more rows in the table.
2 Choose **Edit D**elete Row.
3 Click on the OK button to delete the row or rows.

If data is present in the field row(s) you are deleting, Microsoft Access warns you that the data will be lost if you continue with the deletion.

> **Shortcut:** Click on the field selector to the left of the field name and press the Delete key.

To select all fields in Table Design view

To select all fields in the active table in Table Design view, choose **E**dit Select **A**ll.

Using Keys

A *key* is an index on one or more fields in a table. Indexing records with a key makes retrieving data much faster.

A *primary key* is an index set on a field or group of fields that identifies each record as being unique. A table can have only one primary key.

To set a primary key

To make a field or group of fields in a Table Design view a unique identifier for each record in the table:

1 Select a field.

2 Choose **E**dit **S**et Primary Key.

All values in a field that have been designated as a primary key field must be unique; no duplicates are permitted.

 Shortcut: Select a field, then choose the Set Primary Key tool bar button.

Saving Tables

After creating a table or modifying the design of an existing table, you must save your work if you want your changes in effect the next time you open the database.

To save a table's structure and design

To save modifications to an existing database table's structure and design in Table Design view, choose **F**ile **S**ave.

The Save command saves only the design, not the table data.

Shortcut: Press Shift+F12.

Copying Tables

You may want to make changes to the design of an existing table and retain the original. You can save a copy of a table's design under a different table name and edit each table's design independently.

To make a copy of the current table with a new name

To save the structure and design of a new database table, or to create a copy of the active database table and save it under a new name:

1 Choose File Save As. The Save As dialog box appears.

2 In the Name text box, enter a name for the database object you are saving.

3 Click on the OK button to close the dialog box.

> **Shortcut:** Press F12.

This command copies only the table design in the table you are saving, not the table data.

Switching Views

When you design a table, you can switch between Table Design view and Datasheet view. Switching views enables you to see the effect of any modifications you have made.

To switch to a table's datasheet

To display the data from a table in rows and columns so that many records are visible at one time, choose View Datasheet.

When the table is in the Datasheet view, a check mark appears next to this menu item.

> **Shortcut:** Click on the Datasheet View tool bar button.

To switch to Table Design view

To switch to a Table Design view so that you can create or modify the table's structure, choose View Table Design.

When the table is in Table Design view, a check mark appears next to this menu item.

 Shortcut: Click on the Design View tool bar button.

Properties

Access enables you to set certain table *properties* including a description of the table, a multiple-field primary key, and a multiple-field index. Define table properties on the property sheet from the Design view.

To set a table's properties

To view or change properties for the entire table:

1 Choose View Table Properties. The Table Properties dialog box appears.

2 Enter a description for the table in the Description text box. This description, which can contain up to 255 characters, appears in the status bar whenever this table is current.

3 In the Primary Key text box, enter the name of the field that you want Microsoft Access to use as a primary key for this table.

4 Enter the name of two to five fields to be used as multiple indexes in text boxes Index1–Index5.

5 Close the dialog box by choosing Close from the Control Menu box or pressing Ctrl+F4.

 Shortcut: Click on the View Table Properties button.

Relationships

When you want to tie the information in two different tables together, you can define a relationship between them. You can specify a relationship between the primary key of one table and a field in a second table of the same data type.

To define a relationship between tables

To define a relationship between tables in your database:

1 Choose **E**dit **R**elationships when the Database Window is current. The Relationships dialog box appears.

2 Select the first table from the **P**rimary Table list.

3 To create a one-to-one relationship, select the **O**ne option button in the Type group.

4 To create a one-to-many relationship, select the **M**any option button in the Type group.

5 Select a table name for the second table from the **R**elated table list.

6 From the Select Matching **F**ields list, select a field that matches the data type of the first table's primary key, or select the **Suggest** button if you want Microsoft Access to choose a field in the related table that matches the primary key field of the primary table.

7 To cause Microsoft Access to enforce rules for referential integrity between the first and second tables, select the Enforce Referential Integrity check box.

8 Select the **A**dd button to create the relationship or select the **D**elete button to delete a relationship.

9 Select the **C**lose button to exit the Relationships dialog box.

You can only define relationships between tables that are not open.

Closing Table Design or Datasheet View

When you are finished modifying the table's design or entering data via the table's datasheet, you can close the window to make room for other windows on-screen.

To close Table Design or Datasheet view

To close the active Table Design view without exiting Microsoft Access, choose **F**ile **C**lose.

4

Attaching, Importing, and Exporting Tables

Often you are interested in data that is already stored in another Access database or on disk in a format other than Access' native format. So that you don't have to enter all the data again, Access enables you to import data from other Access databases as well as data created by other programs. This chapter explains how to attach tables from within Access, and how to import and export data to and from tables created by programs other than Access.

Attaching Tables

You can access data from another Microsoft Access database or data that is in a table that was created by another database program by attaching that table to the current database. You can continue to use the attached tables for both applications.

To attach a table

To link a table from an external database to a Microsoft Access database:

1 Choose File Attach Table. The Attach dialog box appears.

2 Choose from the Data Source list the type of external database table you want to attach to your database. The Select File or Database dialog box appears.

3 If only one person at a time is meant to access this file, select the Exclusive check box for improved performance.

4 Enter the name of a database file in the File Name text box, or select a file from the file list, and click on the OK button. The Attach Tables dialog box appears.

5 Select a table from the list in the Tables In list box, and choose the Attach button to link the table to your database. Microsoft Access informs you whether the table was successfully attached. Repeat for as many tables as you need to attach.

6 Choose the Close button after you finish attaching tables.

If the external database table has separate index files, Microsoft Access may prompt you to specify them.

Importing Data

Microsoft Access lets you take data from many different formats and copy it to a table. You may also import a database object from another Microsoft Access database.

To import an Access database

To import a Microsoft Access database:

ATTACHING, IMPORTING, AND EXPORTING TABLES

1 Choose **F**ile **I**mport. The Import dialog box appears.

2 Select the type of file you want to import from the **D**ata Sources list and then click on the OK button. The Select File or Database dialog box appears.

3 Enter a database or file name in the File **N**ame text box, or select a name from the file list, and then choose the Import button. The Select Microsoft Access Database dialog box appears.

4 Enter a database name in the File Name text box, or select a name from the file list, and then choose the Import button. The Import Objects dialog box appears.

5 Select the type of Microsoft Access object you want to import from the Object **T**ype list.

6 Select the name of the object you want to import, and then choose the Import button. Repeat as necessary to import other objects, and then choose the Close button.

7 Choose the **S**tructure Only option to import the field structure and properties of a Microsoft Access table without importing any data into the new table.

8 Choose the Structure and **D**ata option to import a table and copy the data it contains.

You must have owner permissions on the object you want to import.

To import delimited text

To import delimited text:

1 Choose **F**ile **I**mport. The Import dialog box appears.

2 Select the type of file you want to import from the **D**ata Sources list and then click on the OK button. The Select File or Database dialog box appears.

3 Enter a database or file name in the File **N**ame text box, or select a name from the file list, and then choose the Import button. The Select File dialog box appears.

4 Enter in the File Name text box the name of the text file you want to import, or select a file from the file list, and then choose the Import button. The Import Text Options dialog box appears.

5 If the delimited text file contains data that you want to use as field names in the first row, select the First Row Contains Field Names check box.

6 Select **A**ppend to Existing Table to append the records imported from the text file to an existing table in the open database. If you select this option, you must select a table name from the list box.

7 Select **C**reate New Table to create a new table in the open database and import data from the text file into it.

8 To set additional options, choose the **O**ptions button. The Import Text Options dialog box expands to reveal more export settings.

9 If you previously created specifications for importing and exporting, select the name of your specification from the Specification **N**ame list.

10 If you are importing a text file that was created by an OS/2 or MS-DOS application, select DOS or OS/2 (PC-8) from the File Type list. Select Windows (ANSI) as a File Type if the text file was created by a Windows application.

11 Select from the Text **D**elimiter combo box the character you want the text file to use as a text delimiter. If the character you need is not in the list, you may enter a character in the Text **D**elimiter text box.

12 Select from the Field **S**eparator list the character the text file uses as a field separator. If the character you need is not in the list, you may enter a character in the Field **S**eparator text box.

13 Select the date format from the Date **O**rder list.

14 Select from the Date Delimiter list the character you want to use to separate date values.

15 Select the Leading Zeros In Dates check box if you want dates to include a leading zero for one-digit values.

16 Select the Four Digit Years check box to display dates with four digits instead of the usual abbreviated two (10/08/1993 instead of 10/08/93, for example).

17 Enter in the Time Delimiter text box the character you want to use to separate time values.

18 Enter in the Decimal Separator text box the character you want to use as a decimal point in fractional numbers.

19 Choose the Save As button to save these specifications. The Save As dialog box appears. Enter a name for your specifications and click on the OK button.

20 Choose the OK button from the Import Text Options dialog box after you finish editing settings.

To import fixed width text

To import fixed width text:

1 Choose File Import. The Import dialog box appears.

2 Select the type of file you want to import from the Data Sources list and then click on the OK button. The Select File or Database dialog box appears.

3 Enter a database or file name in the File Name text box, or select a name from the file list, and then choose the Import button. The Select File dialog box appears.

4 Enter in the File Name text box the name of the text file you want to import, or select a file from the file list, and choose the Import button. The Import Text Options dialog box appears.

5 Select Append to Existing Table to append the records imported from the text file to an existing table in the open database. If you select this option, select a table name from the list box.

6 Select **C**reate New Table to create a new table in the open database and import data from the text file into it.

7 If you have previously created specifications for importing and exporting a fixed width file, select the name of your specification from the Specification **N**ame list.

8 Choose the OK button from the Import Text Options dialog box after you finish editing settings.

To import a spreadsheet file

To import a spreadsheet file:

1 Choose **F**ile **I**mport. The Import dialog box appears.

2 Select the type of file you want to import from the **D**ata Sources list and then click on the OK button. The Select File or Database dialog box appears.

3 Enter a database or file name in the File **N**ame text box, or select a name from the file list, and then choose the Import button. The Select File dialog box appears.

4 Enter in the File Name text box the name of the spreadsheet file you want to import, or select a file from the file list, and choose the Import button. The Import Spreadsheet Options dialog box appears.

5 Select the **F**irst Row contains Field Names check box if the spreadsheet file contains data that you want to use as field names in the first row.

6 Select **C**reate New Table if you want to create a new table in the open database and import data from the text file into it.

7 Select **A**ppend to Existing Table if you want to append spreadsheet data to an existing table, and select a table name from the list. Any records that you append must have the same structure as the table to which you are appending.

ATTACHING, IMPORTING, AND EXPORTING TABLES

8 If you want to import part of a spreadsheet and not the entire spreadsheet, enter the spreadsheet range name, or specify the range of cells that you want to import in the Spreadsheet **R**ange text box.

9 Choose the OK button from the Import Spreadsheet Options dialog box after you finish editing settings.

Exporting Data

When you need to convert data from a Microsoft Access database into another format so that it can be used by another application, you can export to several different formats.

To export a database object for use by another Microsoft Access Database

To copy data or database objects from a Microsoft Access database to a file that can be used by another Microsoft Access database:

1 Choose **F**ile Export. The Export dialog box appears.

2 From the **D**ata Destination list box in the Export dialog box, highlight Microsoft Access and click on the OK button. The Select Microsoft Access Object dialog box appears.

3 The Object Type list box lists all the types of objects in your database that you can export. Select the database object you want to export.

4 If you are exporting a table, you can choose to export the structure and data together, or you can export only the structure.

To export structure and data, select the Structure and **D**ata option. To export the structure only, select the **S**tructure only option.

5 Click on the OK button. The Export to File dialog box appears.

6 Enter the name of a database file in the File **N**ame text box, or select a file from the file list, and then click on the OK button. The Export dialog box appears.

7 The name of the object or table you are exporting is highlighted in the Export Object To text box. You may change the object's name by entering a new name in this text box.

8 Click on the OK button.

To export a table to delimited text or fixed width text

If you are exporting to delimited text or fixed width text, follow steps 1 through 5 of the section "Exporting a database object to a file for use by another Microsoft Access database." Then follow these steps:

1 If you want Microsoft Access to include field names in the first row of the text file, select the Store **F**ield Names in First Row check box from the Export Text Options dialog box.

2 To set additional options, click on the **O**ptions button. The Export Text Options dialog box expands to reveal more export settings.

3 Select the name of an export specification from the Specification **N**ame list if you are exporting to a fixed width file.

4 If you are exporting to a text file that must be compatible with an OS/2 or MS-DOS application, select DOS or OS/2 (PC-8) from the File Type list. If the text file is for use with a Windows application, select Windows (ANSI) as a File Type.

5 Select from the Text **D**elimiter combo box the character you want the text file to use as a text delimiter. If the character you need is not in the list, you may enter a character in the Text **D**elimiter text box.

6 Select from the Field **S**eparator list the character for the text file to use as a field separator. If the character you need is not in the list, you may enter a character in the Field **S**eparator text box.

ATTACHING, IMPORTING, AND EXPORTING TABLES   57

7 Select the date format from the Date Order list.

8 Select from the Date Delimiter list the character you want to use to separate date values.

9 Select the Leading Zeros In Dates check box if you want dates to include a leading zero for one-digit values.

10 Select the Four Digit Years check box to display dates with four digits instead of the usual abbreviated two (10/08/1993 instead of 10/08/93, for example).

11 Enter in the Time Delimiter text box the character you want to use to separate time values.

12 Enter in the Decimal Separator text box the character you want to use as a decimal point in fractional numbers.

13 Choose the Save As button to save these specifications. The Save Specification As dialog box appears. Enter a name for your specifications and click on the OK button.

14 Choose the OK button from the Export Text Options dialog box to complete the export of the file.

To set up import and export specifications for text files

To create or edit specifications for importing and exporting text files:

1 Choose File Imp/Exp Setup. The Import/Export Setup dialog box appears.

2 Select an existing import/export specification to edit from the Specification Name list, or leave this field blank to create a new specification.

3 If you want to import or export a text file that must be compatible with an OS/2 or MS-DOS application, select DOS or OS/2 (PC-8) from the File Type list. If the text file is for use with a Windows application, select Windows (ANSI) as a File Type.

4 Select from the Text **D**elimiter combo box the character you want the text file to use as a text delimiter. If the character you need is not in the list, you may enter a character in the Text **D**elimiter text box.

5 Select from the Field **S**eparator list the character for the text file to use as a field separator. If the character you need is not in the list, you may enter a character in the Field **S**eparator text box.

If you want to use this specification to import or export fixed-width text files, you must enter field information for each field you want to import or export, as described in the following steps:

1 Enter in the Field Name column the field's name in the Microsoft Access table.

2 Enter in the Data Type column the field's data type in the table.

3 Enter in the Start column the field's starting position (column) in the text file.

4 Enter in the Width column the field's width (number of characters) in the text file.

5 Select the date format from the Date **O**rder list.

6 Select from the Date D**e**limiter list the character you want to use to separates date values.

7 Select the Leading **Z**eros In Dates check box if you want dates to include a leading zero for one-digit values.

8 Select the Four Digit **Y**ears check box to display dates with four digits instead of the usual abbreviated two (10/08/1993 instead of 10/08/93, for example).

9 Enter in the Time Deli**m**iter text box the character you want to use to separate time values.

10 Enter in the Decimal Se**p**arator text box the character you want to use as a decimal point in fractional numbers.

ATTACHING, IMPORTING, AND EXPORTING TABLES **59**

11 Choose the Save As button to save these specifications. The Save As dialog box appears.

12 Enter a name for your specifications, and then click on the OK button.

13 Choose the OK button from the Import/Export Setup dialog box after you finish editing settings.

5

Working with Datasheets

Microsoft Access allows you to look at your data in a variety of ways. Sometimes the information in a record is easier to understand if the record's fields are arranged on a form or a report in a visually pleasing way, sometimes you need to see the maximum number of data records possible on your screen. Datasheet view makes the latter possible.

You can use a datasheet to enter data into a table, although the use of a data entry form makes data entry easier.

Datasheets

A datasheet displays the data in a table, query, or form in multiple rows of records. The field names are displayed across the top of the screen as column headings.

Table datasheets contain the complete set of data that exists in the table. Query datasheets and form datasheets are slightly different in that they are based on dynasets of records.

A form can have one or more underlying tables. The datasheet of a form will display records made up of fields that the form contains, even though the fields may come from different tables. The number of records in the form's dynaset may change if a filter is applied to the data.

A query can have one or more underlying tables. The datasheet of a query will display records made up of the fields that were specified in the QBE grid, and the number of records in the query's dynaset may change depending on the criteria used for the query.

If a datasheet holds more records than will fit on-screen, you can view them by pressing the Page Up and Page Down keys, the up- and down-arrow keys, or clicking on the vertical scroll bar.

If the records contain more fields than you can see on-screen at once, you can see their contents by pressing the Tab or Shift+Tab keys, the left- and right-arrow keys, or by clicking on the horizontal scroll bar.

The number of records that will fit on-screen depends on the default display font that is in effect for the datasheet. For more information on customizing Access, see Chapter 1, "Microsoft Access Basics."

Viewing Datasheet Records

You may switch to datasheet view look at the data in a table, form, query. If the query's properties were set to allow all users to run it with the owner's permission, you can switch to its datasheet; if not, your access is blocked. You can set a form's properties to allow Form view, Datasheet view, or both.

To show all records

To display all current records in a datasheet, choose **R**ecords **S**how All Records.

If you are in Data-entry mode, existing records are hidden from view, and only new records are shown as you enter them. Use the **S**how **A**ll Records command to restore the display.

When you use the **S**how **A**ll Records command to view the datasheet of a form, all filters will be canceled. To restore, run the filter again.

To switch to a datasheet from Design view

To display data records from the current table, form, or query in rows and columns, choose **V**iew Data**s**heet.

 Shortcut: Click on the Datasheet View tool bar button.

Adding a New Record

Although forms offer a more attractive and more flexible environment for data entry than a datasheet does, there may be times when you want to enter data from Datasheet view.

You can enter data in a datasheet, even if it is a form datasheet or a query datasheet.

To enter new records in a datasheet

To jump to a blank record at the end of your form or datasheet so that new records can be added, choose **R**ecords **D**ata Entry.

Shortcut: Press Ctrl+Plus Sign (+).

When you choose the **D**ata Entry command, all existing records are hidden, and a new blank record appears at the top of the screen. Only new records are displayed as they are entered. To end Data-entry mode and view all records, choose the **S**how **A**ll Records command.

The **D**ata Entry command is not available for a read-only datasheet.

To specify whether data entry or changes are allowed in a datasheet

To specify whether the records in a datasheet can be entered or existing data records changed, choose **R**ecords **E**diting Allowed.

This command is a toggle; if editing is currently allowed, a check mark appears next to this menu item. If editing is currently disallowed, no check mark appears.

Moving between Records

Microsoft Access provides you with several ways to move through a datasheet to inspect or change records.

To jump to the first record
To jump from a field in the current record to the same field in the first record, choose **R**ecords **G**o To **F**irst.

> **Shortcuts:** Press Ctrl+Home.
>
> Click the First Record navigation button at the bottom of the Datasheet window.

To jump to the last record
To jump from a field in the current record to the same field in the last record, choose **R**ecords **G**o To **L**ast.

> **Shortcuts:** Press Ctrl+End.
>
> Click the Last Record navigation button at the bottom of the Datasheet window.

To jump to the next record
To jump from a field in the current record to the same field in the next record, choose **R**ecords **G**o To **N**ext.

> **Shortcuts:** Press the down-arrow key.
>
> Click on the Next Record navigation button at the bottom of the Datasheet window.

To jump to the previous record

To jump from a field in the current record to the same field in the previous record, choose **R**ecords **G**o To **P**revious.

> **Shortcuts:** Press the up-arrow key.
>
> Click the Previous Record navigation button at the bottom of the Datasheet window.

Multiuser Data Entry

Using Microsoft Access in a multiuser environment has some special considerations. There is a possibility that one or more users could be viewing and making changes to a database at the same time (if the database is not opened as read-only or for one user's exclusive use). Microsoft Access automatically checks for changes at a specified interval and refreshes or updates each open copy of a database. For more information on customizing Access, see Chapter 1, "Microsoft Access Basics."

To update records in network or multiuser environment

To update all records in the current datasheet or form with any changes made to the data by others in a network or multiuser environment, choose **R**ecords **R**efresh.

The **R**ecords **R**efresh command displays edits and deletions but does not display any new records added by other users.

The **R**ecords **R**efresh command has no effect in a single-user environment.

The Clipboard

The Windows Clipboard is part of the Windows operating environment. You can copy various types of information to the Clipboard and paste it into the same applications or into applications that can display the format of the copied data.

You can use the Clipboard to cut and paste records, fields, text, controls, and entire database objects.

To copy data to the Clipboard
To copy data to the Windows Clipboard:

1 Select the data you want to copy. Datasheet records can be selected in several ways:

   Click on the record selector button to the left of the record you want to select.

   or

   Move the cursor to the record you want to select and then choose **E**dit **S**elect Record.

   To select all records at once, choose **E**dit Select **A**ll.

2 Choose **E**dit **C**opy.

> **Shortcut:** Press Ctrl+C or Ctrl+Ins.

The Windows Clipboard continues to hold the data you copied until you perform another Edit Copy or Edit Cut. The new data replaces all prior data in the Clipboard.

To move data to the Clipboard
To move selected data from the database to the Windows Clipboard:

1 Select the data that you want to move. Datasheet records can be selected in several ways:

Click on the record selector button to the left of the record you want to select.

or

Move the cursor to the record you want to select and then choose **Edit S**elect Record.

To select all records at once, choose **E**dit Select **A**ll.

2 Choose **E**dit **C**ut.

> **Shortcut:** Press Shift+Del or Ctrl+X.

The Windows Clipboard continues to hold the data you cut until you perform another Edit Cut or Edit Copy. The new data replaces all prior data in the Clipboard.

To move data from the Clipboard to the datasheet

To move data from the Windows Clipboard to the datasheet:

1 Select the place that you want to paste previously copied data.

2 Choose **E**dit **P**aste.

> **Shortcut:** Press Ctrl+V or Shift+Ins.

To use **E**dit **P**aste, you must first have placed data in the Windows Clipboard.

You cannot paste data into a database object if the object is marked as read-only.

Removing Data

In Datasheet View of a table, query, or form, you may select one or more records or rows for deletion.

To remove selected data

To remove or delete selected data from the datasheet without putting a copy of the data into the Windows Clipboard:

1 Select the data that you want to remove. Datasheet records can be selected in several ways:

   Click on the record selector button to the left of the record you want to select.

   or

   Move the cursor to the record you want to select and then choose **Edit Select** Record.

   To select all records at once, choose **Edit** Select **All**.

2 Choose **Edit Delete**.

> **Shortcut:** Press Del.

Choosing **D**elete does not copy any data to the Windows Clipboard.

Appending Records

You can use the Clipboard to move records from one datasheet to another or to change the order of records in a datasheet. If you are appending records to a different datasheet from the one the records were copied from, make sure that the two tables agree in number, type, and order of fields.

To append records

To append one or more records to the end of the current datasheet from the Clipboard, choose **E**dit Paste Append.

Data records must previously have been placed in the Windows Clipboard for this command to be available on the menu.

Undo

The Undo/Redo command can help you recover from the effects of a command whose effect was not desired. The command is a toggle; it is effective only on the last action or command that was issued. After you choose this option, it changes to Redo, in effect "undoing" the Undo operation.

To undo or redo an action or command

To reverse the effect of the last action or command, choose **E**dit **U**ndo. To repeat, or redo, the last action or command, choose **E**dit Re**d**o.

> **Shortcuts:** Press Ctrl+Z or Alt+Backspace for both the Undo and Redo commands.
>
> Click on the Undo tool bar button to toggle the effect of the Undo and Redo commands.

Objects and OLE

OLE stands for Object Linking and Embedding. An OLE object is the product of an application that supports linking and embedding. Pictures, sound or video, graphs, and other useful objects can be created in an OLE server application for use by Microsoft Access, the OLE client. An object can be an entire file or a portion of a file that exists separately from your database, in which case a link can be created to the object. An OLE object can also be created and stored in a field of a table, in which case it is referred to as embedded.

You can use OLE in two ways in Microsoft Access. You can link the object. It then is stored in a separate file and modified by the application that created it. The link ensures that any changes made to the file appear in the field to which it is linked.

You can also embed the OLE object. Embedded objects are not stored as separate files. Embedded objects are not available to applications outside of Microsoft Access.

With either method, you can edit the OLE object by selecting it and pressing the Return key, or double-clicking it with the mouse. This starts up the application that created the object and loads it for editing.

OLE objects in tables can be linked to controls on forms and reports. For an example of how pictures can be embedded in a database and displayed on a form, view the Employees Form in the sample NorthWind Database that is shipped with Microsoft Access.

To insert an object into a datasheet

To embed an object from an OLE (Object Linking and Embedding) application into a designated field in the current table's datasheet:

1 Select a field that you have designated to hold an OLE object.

2 Choose Edit Insert Object. The Insert Object dialog box appears.

3 Choose the kind of object you want to embed from the types listed in the Object Type list. The server application starts up. You may then create a new object with the application, or load in an existing file. When you exit the server application, Microsoft Access asks whether you want to update the field with the changed information. Click on the OK button to update the field.

4 You may also choose the File button to insert an object from a file. The Insert Object From File dialog box appears.

5 Select a file type from the List Files Of Type list box.

6 Enter the file name in the File Name text box, or select a file name from the file list.

7 Click on the OK button to close the dialog box and insert the file as an object.

Embedding Objects

An embedded object is not connected to any external file. All the information the OLE object contains is stored within the OLE field.

To embed an OLE object and specify its display format

To link or embed an OLE object into your current datasheet and to select the format in which the object's data will be displayed:

1 Copy the data you want to embed from the source application to the Windows Clipboard by choosing Edit Copy.

2 Select an OLE object field in a datasheet.

3 Choose Edit Paste Special. The Paste Special dialog box appears.

4 Select from the Data Type list the data type to which you want to paste the copied data.

5 Choose the Paste button to embed the object you previously copied from a source application.

Edit Paste, Edit Paste Link, and Edit Paste Special are *grayed out*, or not available on the menu until you first copy the object you want to paste to the Clipboard.

To change an embedded object to a picture

To break the link to a selected OLE object, and modify it so that it can be viewed but can no longer be edited from the original application:

1 Select an embedded object.

2 Choose Edit Object Change to Picture.

To edit an embedded OLE object

To view and modify an OLE object in a datasheet by using its source application:

1 Select an OLE object.

2 Choose Edit Object Edit.

> **Shortcut:** Double-click on the OLE field.

Linking Objects

An OLE link between a field and an external file (or portion of a file) can be defined. Only information about the source of the link is stored in the OLE field.

To create an OLE link
To create a link from an OLE object to a field in the current datasheet:

1 Copy the data you want to link from the source application to the Windows Clipboard by first selecting the data you want to link and then choosing Edit Copy.

2 Select an OLE object field.

3 Choose Edit Paste Link. The Paste Link dialog box appears.

4 Select the Auto Update check box if you want to automatically update all changes from the linked object's source file.

5 Click on the OK button.

Edit Paste, Edit Paste Link, and Edit Paste Special are *grayed out*, or not available on the menu, if the server application does not support linking, or until you first copy the object you want to paste to the Clipboard.

To update an OLE linked object
To update all data in the selected linked OLE object:

1 Select an OLE object.

2 Choose Edit Object Update Now.

To change an OLE link

To update the link from a source application to an OLE object in a datasheet if the original document has been moved or its name has been changed:

1 Choose **E**dit **O**bject Change Link. The Change Link dialog box appears.

2 Select a drive and directory, and enter a file name in the File **N**ame text box or select a name from the file list.

3 Click on the OK button to change the link.

Selecting Records

It's a good practice to select the field(s) or record(s) you want to work with at the start, and then select the operation you want to perform.

To select a record

To select and highlight all the fields in a single record, choose **E**dit **S**elect Record.

> **Shortcuts:** Press Shift+space bar.
>
> Click on the Record Selector button to the left of the record you want to select.

To select all records

To select and highlight every record in a datasheet or a form so that you work with them as a single record, choose **E**dit Select All Records.

> **Shortcut:** Press Ctrl+Shift+space bar.

Saving Changes To a Record

In most cases, Microsoft Access automatically saves any changes that you have made as soon as you move the cursor from the edited record. You can choose to save the record manually, before leaving the edited record, however.

To save changes to the current record

To save any changes that have been made to data in the current record in a datasheet, choose File Save Record.

> **Shortcut:** Press Shift+Enter.

Searching

You can search a datasheet for a record that contains specified text. If you know which field the text will occur in, you can narrow the search to a single field, which speeds searches in large datasheets.

To search for data in a datasheet

To search for data in the current table datasheet:

1 If you want to narrow your search to a single field, tab to the field or select it with your mouse. Choose Edit Find. The Find In Field dialog box appears.

2 Enter the text string that you want to search for in the Find What text box.

3 Select one of the search methods from the three choices in the Where drop-down list.

Any Part of Field searches for any incidence of the text within a field.

Match Whole Field matches the text only when it is identical to the complete contents of a field.

Start of Field searches for the text string at the beginning of a field, but not within it.

4 Select the Current Field option button in the Search In group to search through all of the records, checking only the field that was current when you started the search process.

or

Select the All Fields option button in the Search In group to search all the fields throughout the entire table.

5 Select the Up option button in the Direction group to search backwards from the current record toward the first record.

or

Select the Down option button in the Direction group to search forward from the current record toward the last record.

6 Select the Match Case check box to search for the string exactly as you entered it in the Find What section, matching capitalization.

7 Select the Search Fields as Formatted check box to check for a match with data as it will appear when formatted.

8 Select the Find First button to locate the first occurrence of the text that you are searching for in the table.

9 Select the Find Next button to locate the next occurrence of the text that you are searching for after the current position in the table.

10 Choose the Close button to close the dialog box.

To search for and replace a data string in a datasheet

To search for a string of text in the current table and optionally replace it with another string:

1. If you want to narrow your search to a single field, tab to the field or select it with your mouse. Choose **E**dit **R**eplace. The Replace In Field dialog box appears.

2. Enter the text that you want to replace the first text with in the Re**p**lace With text box.

3. Select the search method from the three choices in the W**h**ere drop-down list.

   Any Part of Field searches for any incidence of the text within a field.

   Match Whole Field matches the text only when it is identical to the complete contents of a field.

   Start of Field searches for the text string at the beginning of a field, but not within it.

4. Select the Current Field option button in the Search In group to search through all of the records, checking only the field that was current when you started the search process.

   or

   Select the All Fields option button in the Search In group to search all the fields throughout the entire table.

5. Select the **U**p option button in the Direction group to search backwards from the current record toward the first record.

   or

   Select the **D**own option button in the Direction group to search forward from the current record toward the last record.

6. Select the Match **C**ase check box to search for the string exactly as you entered it in the Fi**n**d What section, matching capitalization.

7. Select the Search Fields as Fo**r**matted check box to cause Microsoft Access to check for a match with data as it will appear when formatted.

8 Select the Find Next button to locate and highlight, but not replace, the first occurrence of the text string for which you are searching.

9 Select the Replace button to replace the text in the current field after a match is found.

10 Select the Replace All button to have Microsoft Access locate all instances of the search string and replace them with the specified text, without confirming each replacement.

11 Choose the Close button to close the dialog box.

Row Height

The height of rows in a new datasheet is determined by the default display font for the datasheet. You can override the default using the Layout Row Height command. For more information on customizing Access and datasheet options, see Chapter 1, "Microsoft Access Basics."

To change the height of rows in the active datasheet

To change the height of all rows in a datasheet:

1 Choose Layout Row Height. The Row Height dialog box appears.

2 Enter the new height of the row (measured in points) in the Row Height text box.

3 To reset the row height to the Microsoft Access default, select the Standard Height check box. (Standard Height is determined by the point size of the current display font.)

4 Click on the OK button to close the Row Height dialog box.

You also can resize a row manually by using the mouse to drag the lower border of the field selector to the desired width.

You cannot save changes to row height in a Query datasheet.

Column Width

The width of columns in a new datasheet is determined by the default specified in general datasheet options. You can override the default using the **L**ayout **C**olumn Width command. For more information on customizing Access and datasheet options, see Chapter 1, "Microsoft Access Basics."

To change datasheet column width

To change the width of the selected column in a datasheet:

1 Select a column in the datasheet.

2 Choose **L**ayout **C**olumn Width. The Column Width dialog box appears.

3 Enter the width of the column in the **C**olumn Width text box (measured in screen characters).

4 To set the column width to the Microsoft Access default, select the **S**tandard Width check box. (Standard Width is approximately one screen inch.)

5 Click on the OK button to close the Column Width dialog box.

You also can resize a column manually by using the mouse to drag the right border of the field selector to the desired width.

You cannot save column width changes in a Query window.

Hidden Columns

You can temporarily remove one or more fields of data from view without running a filter or query with the **H**ide Columns command.

To hide selected columns

To temporarily remove selected datasheet columns from view:

1 Select one or more columns by placing the cursor anywhere in a column, or by clicking the column selector at the top of the window with your mouse.

2 Choose **L**ayout **H**ide Columns.

The **E**dit **C**opy, **E**dit **P**aste, **E**dit **F**ind, and **E**dit **R**eplace commands do not have any effect on hidden columns.

You cannot save changes to a column display in a Query window.

To show a hidden column

To display a column in the current datasheet:

1 Choose **L**ayout **S**how Columns. The Show Columns dialog box appears.

2 Examine the Co**l**umn list. Currently displayed column or field names have a check mark next to them; currently hidden column or field names have no check mark.

3 Select a column or field name from the Co**l**umn list.

4 Select the **S**how button.

5 Click on the **C**lose button to close the dialog box.

You cannot save changes to a column display in a Query datasheet.

Frozen Columns

When you have a datasheet with many fields, you can opt to freeze one or more columns at the left side of the screen, which prevents them from scrolling out of view when you scroll horizontally.

To freeze columns

To stop selected columns from scrolling off the screen:

1 Select one or more columns.

2 Choose **L**ayout **F**reeze Columns.

You cannot save changes to a column display in a Query window.

To unfreeze all columns

To unfreeze all columns in a datasheet, choose **L**ayout **U**nfreeze Columns.

The Unfreeze Columns command will not operate on a selected column. When you issue the command, all frozen columns are unfrozen.

You cannot save changes to a column display in a Query window.

Fonts

Use the Layout Font command to change the size, appearance, and typeface used to display data and field names in your datasheet. Multiple font settings are not allowed; one font is used throughout the datasheet.

To change a font

To change the font style of the field names and data in a datasheet:

1 Choose **L**ayout **F**ont. The Font dialog box appears.

2 Select a font name from the **F**ont list, or enter a name in the text box.

3 Select a style for the font from the available styles in the Font St**y**le list.

4 Select a point size for the font from the **S**ize list, or enter a point size in the text box.

5 Select the **U**nderline check box in the Effects group to add an underline to the field names and data.

The row height automatically adjusts to the size of a new font if the Standard Height option is in effect.

You cannot save font changes in a Query window.

Gridlines

Gridlines are faint horizontal and vertical lines that visually separate fields and records into columns and rows. You may choose to display or hide them from view.

To hide or display gridlines on a datasheet

To toggle the display of gridlines on a datasheet, choose **Layout Gridlines**. A check mark appears next to this command if the gridlines are displayed. You cannot save changes to grid display in a Query window.

Closing a Datasheet

When you are finished working with a datasheet, you can close its window to make more room for other windows on-screen.

To close the active datasheet

To close the active table datasheet without exiting Microsoft Access, choose **File Close**.

If you have modified the datasheet since the last time you saved it, Microsoft Access prompts you to save your work before exiting the datasheet.

Saving a Datasheet

When you make changes to the design and layout of a datasheet, save your changes if you want to see them in effect the next time the datasheet is opened.

To save a datasheet layout

To save the layout of a datasheet in the Table window so that the appearance of the datasheet is the same the next time you open that datasheet, choose **File Save Layout**.

Design View

Design view is the place you put together all the elements that go into a form, report, query, or table.

To switch to Table Design view

To switch to the Design view of the current database object so that you can create or modify its structure, choose **View Object Design**.

When the table is in Design view, a check mark appears next to this menu item.

> **Shortcut:** Click on the Design View tool bar button.

Printing

When you need hard copy of your data, you may choose any of various ways to send your data to a printer. Print forms and reports to see visually attractive, formatted output. Print a datasheet to get the maximum information on the least amount of paper.

To select a printer

To select a printer and printer options for printing a table, form, query, report, macro, or module:

1 Choose **File Print Setup**. The Print Setup dialog box appears.

2 To select the default Windows printer, select the Default Printer option button. If other printers are installed, select the Specific Printer option button, and select a printer from the list below the button.

3 To print portrait style, select the Portrait option button in the Orientation group.

or

To print landscape style, select the Landscape option button in the Orientation group.

4 To specify the size of the paper on which you are printing, select a size from the Size list in the Paper group.

5 Specify the paper source for your printer by selecting a source from the Source list in the Paper group.

6 Select the Data Only option to print only the data in a datasheet, form, or report; borders, graphics, or gridlines do not print.

7 To change the margin settings, enter new values for the margins in the Left, Right, Top, and Bottom text boxes in the Margins group.

8 To specify the default settings for the printer you chose, select the Options button. The options available to you in the dialog box depend on your selected printer. Click on the OK button to return to the Print Setup dialog box.

9 To view additional print options for forms and reports only, select the More button. The Print Setup dialog box expands downward to reveal options 12 through 16 as listed here.

10 To change the number of columns in the output, enter a new value in the Items Across text box.

11 To change the spacing between rows of the output, enter a new value in the Row Spacing text box.

12 To change the spacing between columns of the output, enter a new value in the Column Spacing text box.

13 To print an entire form or report, select the Same As Detail check box. Deselect the check box to print to an area defined by the Width and Height options.

14 To change the width of the print area, enter a new value in the Width text box in the Item Size group.

15 To change the height of the print area, enter a new value in the Height text box in the Item Size group.

16 Select the Horizontal option button in the Item Layout group to print forms and reports in a horizontal layout.

or

Select the Vertical option button in the Item Layout group to print forms and reports in a vertical layout.

17 Click on the OK button to close the Print Setup dialog box.

To print the active datasheet, report, form, or module

To print the active datasheet, report, form, or module:

1 Choose File Print. The Print dialog box appears.

2 To print the entire active datasheet, report, form, or module, select the All option in the Print Range group.

or

To print a selected range, select the Selection option in the Print Range Group.

or

To specify the pages you want to print, select Pages in the Print Range Group and then enter the beginning page in the From text box and the ending page in the To text box.

3 To specify the quality and speed of printing, select an option from the Print Quality list. The print quality options available to you may differ depending on your printer driver.

WORKING WITH DATASHEETS

4 To print to a file instead of a printer, select the Print to File check box. You can select this option if you do not have a printer installed.

5 To specify more than one set of copies, enter a value in the Copies text box.

6 To collate printed copies of a document, select the Collate Copies check box.

7 To change printers and connections, select the Setup button.

8 To begin printing, click on the OK button.

To view a database object on-screen as it will look after it is printed

To view a form, report, table, query, datasheet, or module on screen as it will appear after printed, choose File Print Preview.

 Shortcut: Click on the Print Preview tool bar button.

6

Query by Example

A *query* is a question that you ask about your data. By setting criteria that must be matched, you can create a set of records from one or more tables or queries. You can also have your query perform an action on this data.

Microsoft Access allows you to build your queries by using QBE (Query by Example). Graphical QBE is a powerful technique, yet simple to learn because of its visual nature.

The Query menu replaces any other menu whenever you open or switch to a query window. You can open a query in Design view or in Datasheet view.

Creating a Query

When you use the Query Design view, you can use your mouse to drag fields from one or more tables to the lower pane and place them in the QBE grid. The fields that you place in the grid determine what data becomes the query's dynaset.

Select Queries

A Select Query searches through its underlying tables to select records that match the criteria you specified. The selected records are referred to as the query's *dynaset*.

A Select Query does not perform any action on the data in its dynaset; however, you may make changes when you edit the dynaset that will change the underlying tables.

To create a new Select Query in the active database
To create a new Select Query in the active database:

1 Select **File New Query**. The default query is a Select Query. The Add Table dialog box appears.

2 The Add Table dialog box lists all the tables and queries in the active database. Select a name from the **T**able/Query List, and select the **A**dd button to add the selected table or query to the current query.

3 Choose the **C**lose button to close the dialog box after you finish adding tables and queries to the new query.

 Shortcuts: Click on the New Query tool bar button.

 Click on the Query object button in the Database window, and then choose the **N**ew button.

Running a Query

Running a query causes Microsoft Access to ask a question based on your criteria of the records in the underlying table(s) or query.

To run the active query
To run the active query and display the data from the current query in rows and columns (Datasheet view), select **Q**uery **R**un.

QUERY BY EXAMPLE

 Shortcuts: Click on the Run Query tool bar button.

Choose View Datasheet.

 Click on the Datasheet View tool bar button.

In Select and Crosstab queries, running the query is the same as clicking on the Datasheet View button.

If the query is in Datasheet view, a check mark appears next to this menu item.

The **R**un command isn't available in a query's Datasheet view.

To switch to Query Design view

To switch from Datasheet View to the Design View of a query to create or modify its structure, choose **V**iew Query **D**esign.

 Shortcut: Click on the Design View tool bar button.

If the query is in Design view, a check mark appears next to this menu item.

Saving a Query in Design View

After adding tables and selecting fields for criteria, you must save the query if you want to use it again. Saving the query saves only the design of the query, it does not save any data.

To save a query's structure and design

To save the structure and design of a query in Design view, choose **F**ile **S**ave.

Choosing the Save command does not save the record data in a query.

> **Shortcut:** Press Shift+F12.

To save a new database object or make a copy of the current object with a new name

To save the structure and design of a new query in Design view or to create a copy of the active query and save the copy under a new name:

1 Select **F**ile Save **A**s. The Save As dialog box appears.

2 Enter a name for the query you are saving in the Query **N**ame text box.

3 Click on the OK button to close the dialog box.

> **Shortcut:** Press F12.

Saving a Query in Datasheet View

After adding tables and selecting fields for criteria, you must save your query if you want to use it again. Saving the query saves only the design of the query; it does not save any data.

Changes you make to the layout and appearance of the datasheet cannot be saved.

To save a query in Datasheet view

To save changes to the design of an existing query and replace the previous version of the query with the active version, choose **F**ile **S**ave Query.

To save a new database object or make a copy of the current object with a new name

To save the structure and design of a new query in Datasheet view or to create a copy of the active query and save the copy under a new name:

1 Choose **F**ile Save Query **A**s. The Save As dialog box appears.

2 Enter a name for the query you are saving in the Query **N**ame text box.

3 Click on the OK button to close the dialog box.

> **Shortcut:** Press F12.

Changing the Name

You can rename any database object when the Database window is active.

To change the name of a query

To change the name of a query in the current database:

1 From the Database window, highlight the query object you want to rename. Choose File Rena**m**e. The Rename dialog box appears, displaying the original name in the title bar.

2 Enter a new name for the query in the text box, and click on the OK button.

If you change the name of a database object, find and update any references to the object that use the original name so that Microsoft Access can locate the object.

Closing the Design Window

When you are finished adding tables and selecting fields for criteria in a Query Design window, you can close the window to make more room for other windows on-screen.

To close the active query design window

To close the active query design window without exiting Microsoft Access, select **F**ile **C**lose.

Criteria

Criteria are instructions that you give a query to determine which records it will select. You can enter criteria for a query in a criteria row, in the QBE grid in Query Design view.

To enter criteria for a query

To enter criteria for a query:

1 In a query's Design view, use the mouse or arrow keys to place the cursor in the first Criteria cell beneath the field for which you want to set criteria.

2 Enter an expression to be used for creating the dynaset.

3 You may enter multiple criteria in each field column.

After you enter an expression in a criteria field, the expression is translated, using Microsoft Access's syntax.

If you don't include an operator with the expression, the equal sign (=) is assumed.

You can use wild-card characters such as * and ? in an expression to select all records containing text that fits a specific pattern.

Operators

Operators are symbols or words that indicate that some type of calculation or operation is to be performed.

The operators in the expression examples in the following table can be used in criteria expressions in a query.

Enter this Expression	To match these records
="Sample"	Records containing the text Sample
="Sample One" or "Sample Two"	Records containing the text Sample One or Sample Two
=#10/8/56#	Records containing a date equal to October 8, 1956
Between #13-Jan-37# And #5-May-42#	Records containing dates between 13-Jan-37 and 5-May-42, inclusive
In ("Red", "Blue", "Green")	Records that have text matching an item in the set
Not "Cinnamon"	Records containing any text value except Cinnamon
< 500	Records containing a value that is less than 500
>= ([Field Name] * 44)	Records that are greater than or equal to the result of multiplying a value field times 44
Like "G*"	Records with text values starting with the letter G
Like "*ing"	Records with text values that end with ing

continues

Enter this Expression	To match these records
Like "[M-Z]*"	Records whose text values start with letters between M and Z, inclusive

By placing one of the expressions in the preceding table in the criteria row beneath a field included in a query and running the query, you select records corresponding to the values stated in the right column of the table.

Calculations

The displayed value of a calculated field is the result of applying an expression to one or more other fields in the same record. Using calculated fields helps you determine summary information for all records in a dynaset of a query.

You can create a calculated field in a query by placing an expression in the field row of a column.

Calculated fields can perform numeric operations on number values or dates, combine several text values in a text field, or calculate totals for fields using aggregate functions, such as Count, Avg, or Sum.

To create a calculated field in a query

To create a calculated field in a query, enter an expression in a cell in the Field row in the form of *New Field Name: Expression*. In a datasheet, this new field name will be used as a column heading.

Any field name you use in an expression in a calculated field must be a field in one of the tables that you added to the query.

You cannot modify the data in or add data to a calculated field. If you make any changes in the dynaset to the values in fields used in the expression, Microsoft Access automatically updates the values in the calculated field.

To perform a summary calculation on a field in all records of a dynaset

To perform a summary calculation on a field in all records of a dynaset:

1 From the Query Design View, select **View T**otals. The Totals row appears in the QBE grid.

2 In the Total row beneath a selected field, select a summary calculation that is compatible with the data type of the selected field as shown in the table at the end of this section.

3 Select **Q**uery **R**un to run your query.

> **Shortcuts:** Click on the Totals tool bar button in the Query Design window.
>
> Click on the Run tool bar button in the Query Design window.

Summary calculation type	Operates on these data types in the selected field	Effect of calculation
Avg	Counter, Number, Currency, Date/Time, Yes/No	Finds the average of all values in the field.
Min	Counter, Number, Currency, Date/Time, Yes/No, Text	Finds the lowest value in the field.
Max	Counter, Number, Currency, Date/Time, Yes/No, Text	Finds the highest value in the field.

continues

Summary calculation type	Operates on these data types in the selected field	Effect of calculation
Count	Counter, Number, Currency, Date/Time, Yes/No, Text, Memo, OLE object	Counts the number of fields in the dynaset that have a value. Blank fields are not counted.
First	Counter, Number, Currency, Date/Time, Yes/No, Text, Memo, OLE object	Finds the value of this field in the first record in the table.
Last	Counter, Number, Currency, Date/Time, Yes/No, Text, Memo, OLE object	Finds the value of this field in the last record in the table.
Var	Counter, Number, Currency, Date/Time, Yes/No	Finds the variance of values in this field.
StDev	Counter, Number, Currency, Date/Time, Yes/No	Finds the standard deviation of values in this field.
Sum	Counter, Number, Currency, Date/Time, Yes/No	Totals all values for this field.

Grouping Data

You can use the QBE grid to design a query that separates your data into groups (based on your specification) and performs summary calculations on each group.

To perform a summary calculation on a field in a group of records in a dynaset

To perform a summary calculation on a field in a group of records in a dynaset:

1 From the Query Design View, select **V**iew **T**otals. The Totals row appears in the QBE grid.

2 In the Total row beneath the field that you want to group, for example, select Group By. This indicates that you want to group all records with identical values in this field.

3 In the next empty row, select the field that you want to perform a calculation on based on its belonging to the group you defined.

If you are grouping sales records by date, for example, you may want to total sales for each day. In this instance, you select the date field and specify it as a group. In the next column, enter the daily sales field and select the summary calculation Sum in the Total row of that column.

When you run this query Microsoft Access displays a datasheet that lists a single row for each date in one column and the sum of daily sales for each date in the other column.

4 Select **Q**uery **R**un to run your query.

> **Shortcuts:** Click on the Totals tool bar button in the Query Design window.
>
> Click on the Run tool bar button in the Query Design window.

To show or hide the Totals row

To display or hide the Totals row while you run summary calculations on grouped data in a query, select View Totals. If totals are displayed, a check mark appears next to the command.

 Shortcut: Click on the View Totals tool bar button.

Adding and Deleting Rows

The QBE grid displays several rows for entering criteria. You may enter an expression on each row, resulting in the same effect as if you had used the OR operator to enter two or more expressions on one line in a criteria row.

Entering the expression **"Like "L*" or Like "A*" or Like "M*"** in one criteria row causes records with text values starting with the letters L, A, or M to be selected for the dynaset. You can achieve the same effect by entering the following text on successive criteria rows:

"Like "L*"

"Like "A*"

"Like "M*"

When you have many criteria or conditions, you can read them more easily by placing them on separate rows. If you have more criteria than the QBE grid Access provides rows for, you may add as many rows as needed.

To insert a blank criteria row into a query Design window

To create a new, blank criteria row above the selected criteria row in a query, choose Edit Insert Row.

To delete criteria rows from a query

To delete one or more selected criteria rows from a query:

1 Select a row in the query.

2 Select **Edit D**elete Row.

> **Shortcut:** Select a row and press the Delete key.

To clear the current query

To clear the current query by deleting all the fields listed in the grid of a query's Design view, select **E**dit Delete **A**ll. Deleting a field from a query does not delete the field or data in the underlying table(s).

Adding and Removing Tables

A query can create a dynaset from a single table or query, or multiple tables and queries. Every query must have at least one table or query added to it.

To add a table or query to a query

To add tables and queries to the active query:

1 Select **Q**uery Add Table. The Add Table dialog box appears. All the tables and queries in the open database are listed in alphabetical order.

2 Select from the **T**able/Query list the name of the table or query you want to add to the current query.

3 Select the **A**dd button to add the table or query.

4 Choose the **C**lose button to close the dialog box.

You can select only one table or query from the list at a time to add to the current query, but you can add as many tables or queries as you want before closing the dialog box.

You also can add a table or query to the current query by using the mouse to drag the table or query name from the Database window to the upper part of the Query window.

To remove a query or table from a query

To remove a query or a table from a query:

1 Select a table you want to remove by using the F6 key to make the top pane of the Query Design window active and then tabbing to the table or query list you want to select. You also may select a table or query list by clicking on it.

2 Choose **Q**uery **R**emove Table.

After you remove a table from a query, any fields from that table displayed on the QBE grid also are removed.

> **Shortcut:** Select a table or query as explained in the preceding steps, and then press the Delete key.

Joins

When you create a query that is based on multiple tables or queries, you must define how the data from the different sources will be combined in the dynaset. You need to establish a relationship between the tables in the query by joining them. The primary key field in one table is joined to a field of the same data type in another table.

Microsoft Access supports three types of joins: the equi-join, outer join, and self-join.

An *equi-join* combines all the records from both tables that are joined whenever the values in the joined fields are equal.

Two types of outer join exist: the left outer join and the right outer join. An *outer join* includes all records from one table and, from the other table, only records where the joined fields are equal. The *left outer join* selects all records from the first table and matching field records from the second table. The *right outer join* selects all records from the second table and matching field records from the first table.

A *self-join* can be created for a table that has a field related to another field in the same table. You add the same table to a query twice and define the join between the related fields.

You can see a visual representation of the relationship between tables; any joins are shown as lines connecting the joined fields.

To create an equi-join

The equi-join is the default for every join. Use the mouse to drag a column from one table to another table.

You can select the **E**dit **R**elationships command from the Database menu to establish default joins between tables.

To create an outer join

To create an outer join:

1 Create an equi-join by dragging a column from one table to another table.

2 In the QBE section of the Query Design window, select the join line that you want to change to an outer join by clicking on that line. (A selected line becomes bold.)

3 Select **V**iew **J**oin Properties, or double-click on the bold line. The Join Properties dialog box appears.

4 Select option button **1** to include only rows where the joined fields from both tables are equal. This is an equi-join, which is the default.

or

Select option button **2** to include all records from the first table and only those records from the second table where the joined fields are equal. This is a left outer join.

or

Select option button **3** to include all records from the second table and only those records from the first table where the joined fields are equal. This is a right outer join.

To create a self-join
To create a self-join:

1 Add a table to a query twice.

2 Create an equi-join between the related fields in the table by dragging a field from the first instance of the table to the related field in the second instance of the table.

Append Queries

An *Append query* is an action query. When action queries perform an action, they make changes on the records in their underlying tables. You can use an Append query to add selected records from one table or query to the end of another table.

To create an Append query
To copy all records or a specified group of records based on set criteria from one table to another:

1 Create a Select query, adding tables and criteria.

2 Run the Select Query (select **Q**uery **R**un) to make sure that the records selected by your criteria are the ones you want to append to another table.

3 From Query Design view, select **Q**uery **A**ppend. The Query Properties dialog box appears.

4 Select from the Table **N**ame list in the Append To group the name of the table to which you want to append this query, or enter a table name in the Table **N**ame text box.

QUERY BY EXAMPLE 103

5 Select the Current Database option button to append this query to a table in the current database.

or

Select the Another Database option button to append this query's results to a table in another database.

6 If you selected Current Database, skip to step 7. If you selected Another Database, enter the path and database name in the File Name text box. If the other database is not a Microsoft Access database, enter the path and product name in the text box.

7 Select the Unique Values Only check box to instruct Microsoft Access to retrieve only unique data values.

8 Select the Run with Owner's Permissions check box to give users in a network environment with a secure system permission to view the data in the query.

9 Click on the OK button to close the dialog box.

10 Return to Query Design view and select Query Delete. The title bar of the current query changes to reflect the change in query type.

11 Select Query Run to run the Append query and view the dynaset in the datasheet. You may optionally run the query by selecting View Datasheet. The commands are equivalent.

Shortcuts: Run an Append query by clicking on the Run Query tool bar button.

Run an Append query by clicking on the Datasheet View tool bar button.

Records are not appended if duplicate or empty values are in the primary key field.

A check mark appears next to this menu item after the item has been selected.

Crosstab Queries

A *Crosstab query* displays data from one or more tables or queries and summarizes the data in rows and columns, much like the format of a spreadsheet.

When you create a Crosstab query, the Crosstab and Total rows are added to the QBE grid. You must select an option in the Total row for every field in the grid.

You can specify one or more row headings for the Crosstab query. These appear in the left columns of the query datasheet and label the groups that you are summarizing.

You may specify only one field or expression for the column heading. The column heading to be displayed across the top of the query datasheet is determined by the value of the field or expression you selected.

To create a Crosstab query

To create a Crosstab query:

1 Create a new Select query in Query Design view, adding the tables you want to use and defining relationships between the tables, if necessary.

2 Select **Query Crosstab**. The Total row and the Crosstab row appear in the QBE grid.

3 Select the fields you want to use for the crosstab's rows, columns, or computed values, and place these fields in the QBE grid. You can use expressions in place of field names.

4 Select any additional fields for which you need to specify criteria or sort order.

5 Select the Crosstab row in the column for the field whose value you want to use as row headings. Then select Row Heading from the drop-down list box. You can select multiple fields to be used as row headings.

QUERY BY EXAMPLE   105

6 Select the Total row in the column for the field whose value you want to use as row headings. Then select Group By (the default). You can select multiple fields to be used as row headings.

7 Select the Crosstab row in the column for the field whose value you want to use for column headings. Then select Column Heading from the drop-down list box. You may select only one field or expression to be used for column headings.

8 Select the Total row in the column for the field whose value you want to use as column headings. Then select Group By (the default). You may select only one field or expression to be used for column headings.

9 Select the Crosstab row, and then select Value from the drop-down list.

10 Select the Total row in the column for the field whose values you want to calculate and cross-tabulate. Then select the type of aggregate function you want for the cross-tabulation (such as Sum, Avg, or Count) from the drop-down list.

11 Select Where in the Total row for any additional fields for which you want to specify criteria. Then enter an expression in the Criteria row.

Leave the Crosstab row blank for fields in which you specify criteria.

12 Choose **Q**uery **R**un to run the Crosstab query and view the dynaset in the datasheet. You may optionally run the query by choosing **V**iew **D**atasheet. The commands are equivalent.

Shortcuts: Run a Crosstab query by clicking on the Run Query tool bar button.

Run a Crosstab query by clicking on the Datasheet View tool bar button.

A check mark appears next to this menu item after the item has been selected.

To stop execution of a query that is running, press Ctrl+Break.

Delete Queries

A *Delete query* is an action query. Action queries make changes on the records in their underlying tables when they perform an action. You can use a Delete query to remove records from a table based on the criteria that you specify.

To create a Delete query
To create a Delete query:

1 Create a Select query, adding tables and criteria.

2 Run the Select Query (select **Q**uery **R**un) to make sure that the records selected by your criteria are the ones you want to delete.

3 Return to Query Design View and select **Q**uery **D**elete. The title bar of the current query changes to reflect the change in query type.

4 Select **Q**uery **R**un to run the Delete query and view the dynaset in the datasheet. You may optionally run the query by selecting **V**iew **D**atasheet. The commands are equivalent.

  Shortcuts: Run a Delete query by clicking on the Run Query tool bar button.

 Run a Delete query by clicking on the Datasheet View tool bar button.

A check mark appears next to this menu item after the item has been selected.

To stop execution of a query that is running, press Ctrl+Break.

After you run the query and choose OK to confirm the deletion, you cannot undo the delete operation.

Make Table Queries

A *Make Table* query is an action query. When action queries perform an action, they make changes on the records in their underlying tables. You can use a Make Table query to create a new table, based on records selected from the current query's table(s).

To make a new table from a query's dynaset

To make a new table from a query's dynaset:

1 Create a Select query, adding tables and criteria.

2 Run the Select Query (choose **Q**uery **R**un) to make sure that the records selected by your criteria are the ones you want to use to create a new table.

3 Return to Query Design view and choose **Q**uery Ma**k**e Table. The title bar of the current query changes to reflect the change in query type. The Query Properties dialog box appears.

4 Enter a name for the new table in the Table **N**ame text box, or select an existing table name from the drop-down list box to overwrite the data in the selected table with the new data from the dynaset of this query.

5 Select **Q**uery **R**un to run the Make Table query and view the dynaset in the datasheet. Optionally, you may run the query by selecting **V**iew **D**atasheet. The commands are equivalent.

 Shortcuts: Run a Make Table query by clicking on the Run Query tool bar button.

 Run a Make Table query by clicking on the Datasheet View tool bar button.

A check mark appears next to this menu item after the item has been selected.

To stop execution of a query that is running, press Ctrl+Break.

Update Queries

An Update Table query is an action query. Action queries make changes when they perform an action on the records in their underlying tables. You can use an Update Table query to perform the same action on fields in every record of a query's dynaset.

To create an Update query

To create an Update query, select **Q**uery **U**pdate.

1 Create a Select query, adding tables and criteria.

2 Run the Select Query (select **Q**uery **R**un) to check that the records selected by your criteria are the records you want to update.

3 Return to Query Design view and select **Q**uery **U**pdate Table. The title bar of the current query changes to reflect the change in query type. The Update To row appears in the QBE grid of the Update Query window.

4 Select the Update To row in the column of the field you want to update. Enter a value to replace all other values in that field, or enter an expression to be applied to each field.

5 Select **Q**uery **R**un to run the Update Table query and view the resulting dynaset in the datasheet. Optionally, you may run the query by selecting **V**iew **D**atasheet. The two commands are equivalent.

6 A message box appears to tell you how many records will be updated in the table. This message box also requests that you confirm the update. Click on the OK button to proceed with the update.

> **Shortcuts:** Run an Update Table query by clicking on the Run Query tool bar button.
>
> Run an Update Table query by clicking on the Datasheet View tool bar button.

A check mark appears next to this menu item after you select the item.

To stop execution of a query that is running, press Ctrl+Break.

Parameter Queries

A Parameter Query asks you to specify the criteria it needs every time you run the query. If you run a query on a frequent basis, the Parameter Query saves the extra time and work required to change the criteria manually in Query Design view.

To create a Parameter query

To create a Parameter query:

1 Create a Select Query, adding tables as explained earlier in this chapter.

2 Choose Query Parameters. The Query Parameters dialog box appears.

3 In the Parameter column of the Query Parameters dialog box, enter in the statement you want to appear as a prompt when the query is run. This statement must also be entered in the criteria row of the field being queried and enclosed in brackets.

4 In the Query Parameters dialog box, enter the data type of the criteria you are prompting for, or select a type from the drop-down list.

5 Click on the OK button to close the dialog box.

6 Select **Q**uery **R**un to run the Parameter query. Microsoft Access prompts you for the criteria, using the text you entered as a prompt. You may optionally run the query by selecting **V**iew **D**atasheet. The two commands are equivalent.

> **Shortcuts:** Run a Parameter query by clicking on the Run Query tool bar button.
>
> Run a Parameter query by clicking on the Datasheet View tool bar button.

A check mark appears next to this menu item after you select the item.

To stop execution of a query that is running, press Ctrl+Break.

Properties

Each different type of query has its own set of properties. These properties define the default values that a query uses to create a dynaset.

To set a query's properties

To view or change properties for the current query, select **V**iew Query Proper**t**ies. The Query Properties dialog box appears. The type of query that is current determines which query properties are available.

If an Append query is current:

1 Select from the Table **N**ame list in the Append To group the name of the table to which you want to append this query, or enter a table name in the text box.

2 Select the **C**urrent Database option button to append this query to a table in the current database.

or

Select the **A**nother Database option button to append this query's results to a table in another database.

3 If you selected **C**urrent Database, skip to step 4. If you selected **A**nother Database, enter the path and database name of the other database in the **F**ile Name text box. If the database is not a Microsoft Access database, enter the path and product name in the text box.

4 Select the **U**nique Values Only check box to instruct Microsoft Access to retrieve only unique data values.

5 Select the Run with **O**wner's Permissions check box to give users in a network environment with a secure system permission to run the query.

6 Click on the OK button to close the dialog box.

If a Crosstab query is current:

1 You can select the **U**nique Values Only check box to instruct Microsoft Access to retrieve only unique data values. Because you are performing calculations and crosstabbing fields that may have duplicate values, however, this option is not recommended for crosstab queries.

2 Select the Run with **O**wner's Permissions check box to give users in a network environment with a secure system permission to run the data in the query.

3 Select the **F**ixed Column Headings check box to specify the order of the column headings and stabilize the headings for use in a form or report.

4 Enter headings in the **F**ixed Column Headings text box in the order you want the headings to appear in the query's datasheet; separate each heading with a semicolon.

5 Click on the OK button to close the dialog box.

If a Delete query is current, you may select the Run with **O**wner's Permissions check box to give users in a network environment with a secure system permission to run the query.

If a Make Table query is current:

1. Select from the Table Name list in the Append To group the name of the table you want to create to hold the results of this query, or enter a table name in the Table Name text box.

2. Select the Current Database option button to create a table in the current database.

   or

   Select the Another Database option button to create a table in another database.

3. If you selected Current Database, skip to step 4. If you selected Another Database, enter the path and database name of the other database in the File Name text box. If the database is not a Microsoft Access database, enter the path and product name in the text box.

4. Select the Unique Values Only check box to instruct Microsoft Access to retrieve only unique data values.

5. Select the Run with Owner's Permissions check box to give users in a network environment with a secure system permission to run the query.

6. Choose the OK button to close the dialog box.

If a Select query is current:

1. Select the Unique Values Only check box to instruct Microsoft Access to retrieve only unique data values.

2. Select the Run with Owner's Permissions check box to give users in a network environment with a secure system permission to view the data in the query.

3. Select the Restrict Available Fields check box to instruct Microsoft Access to limit the fields listed in the field list to those in the QBE grid.

4. Click on the OK button to close the dialog box.

The Query Properties dialog box opens when you create a Make Table query or an Append query. You may view and change the default query properties as a step in creating the query.

> **Shortcut:** Click on the View Query Properties tool bar button.

When you create a query in the Query Design window, the SQL (Structured Query Language) equivalent of your query is generated by Microsoft Access.

SQL statements can be used in place of expressions, arguments to Access Basic procedures, and property settings.

You can use SQL to query, update, and manage the data in your tables.

To change, view, or create a query's SQL statement

To view, create, or modify a query by using Structured Query Language (SQL):

1 Select View SQL. The SQL dialog box appears.

2 Enter SQL statements in the SQL Text: text box, or modify existing statements.

3 Press Ctrl+Enter to add new lines.

4 Click on the OK button to close the SQL dialog box.

Any changes you make in the SQL dialog box are reflected in your query.

Controlling the Display

Microsoft Access allows you to customize the look of many of its windows.

To display or hide table names that are part of a query in Design view

To toggle the display of the table names in the QBE grid on and off and to keep track of which field is selected from which table in multitable queries, select **V**iew Table **N**ames.

This command is a toggle. To hide the table names, choose the Table **N**ames command again. When table names are currently displayed, a check mark appears next to this menu item.

Saving Changes

In most cases, Microsoft Access automatically saves any changes that you make as soon as you move the cursor from the edited record in a datasheet. However, you can choose to save the record manually, before leaving the edited record.

To save changes to the current record

To save any changes that have been made to data in the current record in a datasheet, choose **F**ile Save Rec**o**rd.

> **Shortcut:** Press Shift+Enter.

Listing Queries

To display the list of queries in the database

To display a list of all the queries in the active database, select **V**iew **Q**ueries.

> **Shortcut:** Select the Query object button in the Database window.

Printing a Query

When you need hard copy of your data, you may choose one of several ways to send your data to a printer. Print forms and reports to see visually attractive, formatted output. Print the Datasheet view of your data to get the maximum information on the least amount of paper.

You can only print the Datasheet view of a table or query. The Print options are not available in Table Design view or Query Design view.

You can print a form in both Datasheet and Form views. Reports can be printed from Design view or Print Preview.

Access Basic modules can only be printed from Design view.

Macros can not be printed.

To print the active query datasheet

To print the active query datasheet:

1 Select File **P**rint. The Print dialog box appears.

2 To print the entire query datasheet, select the **A**ll option in the Print Range group.

   or

   To print a range of records you have selected in the datasheet, select the **S**election option in the Print Range Group.

   or

   To specify the pages you want to print, select **P**ages in the Print Range Group, and then enter the beginning page in the **F**rom text box and the ending page in the **T**o text box.

3 To specify the resolution and speed of the print job, select an option from the Print **Q**uality list. The print quality options may differ, depending on your printer driver.

4 Select the Print to File check box if you want to send output to a file instead of a printer. You can select this option if you don't have a printer installed.

5 If you want to print more than one set of copies, enter a value in the Copies text box.

6 To *collate,* or arrange, the printed pages in complete sets, select the Collate Copies check box.

7 To change printers and connections, select the Setup button. For more information on selecting a printer, see Chapter 5.

8 To begin printing, choose the OK button.

To view a query datasheet on-screen as it will look after it is printed

To view a datasheet on-screen as it will appear after it is printed, select File Print Preview.

 Shortcut: Click on the Print Preview tool bar button.

To select a printer

To select a printer and printer options for printing a query datasheet:

1 Choose File Print Setup. The Print Setup dialog box appears.

2 Select the Default Printer option button if you want to use the default Windows printer. If you have more than one printer installed, you can select the Specific Printer option button, and select a printer from the Specific Printer list.

3 To print portrait style (vertical paper orientation), select the Portrait option button in the Orientation group.

or

To print landscape style (horizontal paper orientation), select the **Landscape** option button in the Orientation group.

4 Select a size from the **Size** list in the Paper group to specify the size of the paper you are printing on.

5 Specify the paper source for your printer by selecting a source from the **Source** list in the Paper group.

6 Select the Data Onl**y** option to separate data from graphic elements in a datasheet, form, or report, and print only the data without any borders, graphics, or gridlines.

7 To change the margin settings, enter new values for the margins in the **L**eft, Ri**g**ht, **T**op, and **B**ottom text boxes in the Margins group.

8 To specify the default settings for the printer you chose, choose the **O**ptions button. The options available to you in the dialog box depend on your selected printer. Click on the OK button to return to the Print Setup dialog box.

9 The **M**ore button will be disabled or *grayed out* unless you are printing a form or report.

10 Click on the OK button to close the Print Setup dialog box.

7

Forms

A Microsoft Access form is a special window that is used for data entry. You can use the visual power of Windows to create an attractive form using a combination of graphics and text. Microsoft Access forms can present your data in a format that is easier to read and understand than a datasheet.

Microsoft Access makes creating attractive forms based on multiple tables or queries easy. Provided with Microsoft Access are FormWizards, special tools that help you create data entry forms by asking you to answer some basic questions about how you want to present your data and then doing the layout work for you. The Form Design view lets you start a form from scratch or customize a form that FormWizard helped you design.

The Form menu appears whenever you open or switch to a Form window. You can open a form in Design view or in Datasheet view.

Creating Forms

You have two options to choose from when you want to create a new report. You can go directly to Form Design view to start with a blank form, or you can have the FormWizard help you design a basic report.

To create a new data entry form

To create a new data entry form:

1 Select **F**ile Ne**w** **F**orm. The New Form dialog box appears.

2 Enter the name of a table or query on which to base the new form, or select a name from the Select a **T**able/Query drop-down list.

3 Select the FormWizards button for step-by-step assistance in creating the form layout you want. If no tables or queries are in your database, the FormWizards button is disabled, or *grayed out.*

or

Select the **B**lank Form button to create a blank Form and immediately enter the Form Design view.

Shortcuts: Click on the New Form tool bar button.

Select the Form object button on the left side of the Database window, and then select the **N**ew button at the top of the Database window.

Using FormWizards

The FormWizards take most of the work out of designing a basic data entry form. Just answer a few simple questions, and the Microsoft Access FormWizards produce an attractive form report based on the tables and queries that you specify.

FormWizards can speed development by quickly giving you a basic form you can customize. Using FormWizards takes far less effort than starting from a blank form.

To use the FormWizard to design your form:

1 Choose **F**ile Ne**w F**orm. The New Form dialog box appears.

2 Enter the name of a table or query on which to base the new form, or select a name from the Select a **T**able/Query drop-down list.

3 Choose the Form**W**izard button. The Microsoft Access FormWizard dialog box appears.

4 You can choose from four FormWizards: Single column, Tabular, Graph, and Main/Subform.

- A *Single-column form* displays the fields from each data record in a single column. Each value is on a separate line, with a descriptive label to its left.

- A *Tabular form* displays data from left to right, much like a datasheet.

- A *graph* is a graphical representation of your data.

- *Main/Subform* creates a data entry form with a subform from another table embedded in it.

Select which style of form you want. Then follow the detailed directions in each dialog box that tell you how to proceed.

5 After you specify the fields to be used in your form, you are asked to select the look of the form. You can choose from Standard format, Chiseled Format, Shadowed format, Boxed format, or Embossed format.

Select the option button next to each and look at the picture of the magnifying glass to see the differences in the appearance of these five formats. Select the **N**ext button when you are through.

6 The Form Title defaults to the name of the table or query that you based it on. To give the report a different name, enter a report name in the Form title text box.

7 The FormWizard is finished. Choose the Open button to see how your new form looks in Form view, or choose the Design button to go to Form Design view, where you can customize your form.

Opening Forms

You can open an existing form in Form view or in Design view to modify its design and the layout of controls.

To open an existing form
To open a form in Design view:

1 From the active Database window, select View Forms, or click on the Form object button. A list of existing reports appears in the Database window.

2 Select the **D**esign button at the top of the Database window.

To open a form in Form view:

1 From the active Database window, select View Forms, or click on the Form object button. A list of existing reports appears in the Database window.

2 Select the **O**pen button at the top of the Database window.

To display the list of forms in the database
To display a list of all the forms in the active database, select View Forms.

 Shortcut: Select the Form object button in the Database window.

Form View

Form view displays a data entry form for inspecting or entering the data in a table or query.

To display a form in Form view

To display a form in Form view so that you can add, delete, update, or view data in the underlying table, select **V**iew **F**orm from the Design view, Datasheet view, or Filter window of an open form.

When the form is in Form view, a check mark appears next to this menu item.

 Shortcut: Click on the Form View tool bar button.

To size a form window to hold the maximum number of complete records

To adjust the size of the Form view window to display the maximum number of complete records, choose **W**indow Si**z**e To Fit Form.

If the window shows only one record and that record is only partially displayed, selecting **W**indow Size To Fit Form enlarges the window to show as much of the record as can fit in the window.

If the displayed record is smaller than the active window, choosing **W**indow Size To Fit Form crops the window to the size of the record.

Datasheet View

You may switch to Datasheet view to look at the data in a form. A form's properties can be set to allow Form view, Datasheet view, or both.

To switch to a form's datasheet

To display the data in the underlying table in rows and columns select **V**iew Data**s**heet.

 Shortcut: Click on the Datasheet View tool bar button.

The form's properties can be set to stop users from switching to Datasheet view.

When the form is in Datasheet view, a check mark appears next to this menu item.

Design View

In Form Design view, you specify which data fields go into your form and how the data will be displayed.

A form is based on a single table or query. If information from a second table or query must be displayed, you can add a subform by dragging the name of the second form from the database window to the form in Design view.

The toolbox is a collection of form controls that you can add. Use the toolbox to add controls to a form. To add a control to your form from the toolbox, click to select the tool, drag the pointer from the toolbox to the desired location in the form in Design view, and then click the mouse again.

To display the current form in Design view

To display a form in Design view so that you can create and modify the structure of a form select **View Form Design** from the Form view or the Datasheet view on an open form.

When the form is in Form Design view, a check mark appears next to this menu item.

 Shortcut: Click on the Form Design View tool bar button.

To hide or display a field list

To toggle the display of a list of the fields in the underlying dynaset of the current form:

1 Select **View Field List**.

2 To close the field list, select **View Field List** again.

FORMS **125**

When the field list is open, a check mark appears next to this menu item.

 Shortcut: Click on the Field List tool bar button in the current Form Design window.

Subform

A *subform* is a control on a form that displays another form. Subforms enable you to combine fields from multiple tables or queries.

To change the display of a subform datasheet

To change how a subform is displayed in the main form, you use the **View S**ubform Datasheet command, which is a toggle. From the active subform, choose **View S**ubform Datasheet once to change the subform display to Form view. Choose it again to change the subform display to Datasheet view.

When the subform is open in Datasheet view, a check mark appears next to this menu item.

Palette Window

The *Palette window* is a small window that "floats" above a form in Design view. Use the Palette window to change the look of a section or control; the background color of a section or control; the visibility, width, and color of a control's border; and the color of the text within a control.

To hide or display the Palette window

To toggle the display of the Palette window in a form's Design view select **View P**alette.

When the Palette window is open, a check mark appears next to this menu item.

> **Shortcut:** Click on the Palette tool bar button.

Ruler

You can use the rulers displayed along the top and left edges of a form in Design view as guides for aligning and placing controls on the form.

To display or hide the left and top ruler display

To toggle the display of the rulers at the top and along the left side of the current form's Design view, select **View R**uler.

When the rulers are displayed, a check mark appears next to this menu item.

Toolbox

The toolbox is a small window that "floats" above a form in Design view. The toolbox contains controls that you can place on the form.

To display or hide the toolbox

To toggle the display of the toolbox in the current form's Design view, select **View T**oolbox.

When the toolbox is currently displayed, a check mark appears next to this menu item.

Selecting Controls

Several menu options exist that enable you to modify a control or group of controls. To have a command operate on a single or multiple controls, you must first select the controls.

To select a control
In Form Design view, press the tab key until the control is selected, or click on the control once.

To select multiple controls
In Form Design view, drag the mouse pointer over the controls you want to select, partially enclosing the controls with the sizing box. Release the mouse button to make your selection final.

To select all the controls on the active form
To select all controls in all sections in the Design view of the active form, select **Edit Select All**.

To select the entire form
To select the entire active form when it is displayed in Design view, select **Edit Select Form**.

Tab Order of Controls

You can use the tab key to move through the controls on a form, both in Design view and Form view. The default order is the order in which the controls were placed on the form.

To specify Tab Order
To specify the order in which the insertion point moves through the fields as you tab through a form in Design or Form view:

1 Select **Edit Ta**b Order. The Tab Order dialog box appears.

2 Select the Form **H**eader option button to set the tab order for the form header section. (This option button is not available if the form has no header.)

3 Select the **D**etail option button to set the tab order for the detail section.

4 Select the Form **F**ooter option button to set the tab order for the form footer section. (This option button is not available if the form has no footer.)

5 Select one or more fields by clicking on the gray button to the left of each field. After a field or fields are selected, click on the selected area again and drag the fields to a new position.

6 Select the **A**uto Order button to instruct Microsoft Access to set the tab order from left to right, and top to bottom.

7 Click on the OK button to close the Tab Order dialog box and set the new tab order.

Aligning Controls

You can easily add controls to a Microsoft Access form by dragging and placing the controls, by using the mouse. For example, sometimes you may want to neaten the form you created if controls do not line up in a column or row.

To align controls with the left edge of the leftmost control

To align selected controls on the current form with the left edge of the leftmost selected control:

1 Select controls on the active form.

2 Select **L**ayout **A**lign **L**eft.

To align controls with the bottom edge of the bottommost control

To align selected controls on the current form with the bottom edge of the bottommost selected control:

1 Select controls on the active form.

2 Choose **L**ayout Align **B**ottom.

To align controls with the right edge of the rightmost control

To align selected controls on the current form with the right edge of the rightmost selected control:

1 Select controls on the active form.

2 Choose **L**ayout Align **R**ight.

To align the top left corners of the selected controls

To align the top left corners of the selected controls to the nearest grid point on the active form:

1 Select controls on the active form.

2 Choose **L**ayout Align To **G**rid.

To align controls with the top edge of the topmost control

To align selected controls on the current form with the top edge of the topmost selected control:

1 Select controls on the active form.

2 Choose **L**ayout Align **T**op.

To create a copy of a control that is evenly aligned and spaced

To create an evenly spaced and aligned copy of a selected control:

1 Select a control on the form in Design view.

2 Choose **E**dit **D**uplicate.

Bring to Front, Send to Back

If you place many controls on a form, they can overlap, making covered controls partially or completely invisible. You can select one or more hidden controls with the mouse or the tab key. Then you can bring the controls to the top of a stack of controls that overlap each other or move the selected controls to the bottom of a stack of controls that overlap each other.

To bring selected controls to the top of overlapping controls

To bring selected controls to the top of overlapping controls:

1 Select one or more controls on a form in Design view.

2 Choose Layout Bring To Front.

To send selected controls to the back of overlapping controls

To send selected controls to the back of overlapping controls:

1 Select one or more controls on a form in Design view.

2 Choose Layout Send To Back.

The Form Design Grid

The grid helps you place and align controls on a form in Form Design view.

To display or hide the Grid in Design view

To display or hide the grid in the current form's Design view, select View Grid. This command is a toggle. When the grid is currently displayed, a check mark appears next to this menu item.

The form's Grid X and Grid Y properties determine how closely together the grid dots are. Both properties must be less than 17 in order for the grid to be visible.

To snap selected controls to grid alignment

To adjust the size of selected controls so that their sides align to the nearest points on the grid:

1 Select one or more controls.

2 Choose **L**ayout Size To **G**rid.

Size to **G**rid works even if the grid is not displayed.

To specify that all new or modified controls align to the grid

To specify that new controls align to the grid as you add, move, or resize these controls on a form in Design view, select **L**ayout **S**nap To Grid. Selecting this item more than once toggles **S**nap To Grid on and off. A check mark appears next to this menu item if it is enabled.

Sizing Controls

Sometimes a control is not big enough to completely display the data it contains. You can resize a control in the Form Design window of a form.

To size selected controls to display their contents

To adjust the height and width of a control so that the text the control contains is visible:

1 Select one or more controls that contain text in the Design view of the current form.

2 Select **L**ayout Si**z**e To Fit.

Properties

Database objects have a set of properties that determines how the object looks and works.

To display a form's property sheet

To display or hide the property sheet in a form's Design view so that you can inspect and modify properties for the form and its controls, choose View Properties.

When the Properties window is open, a check mark appears next to this menu item.

 Shortcut: Click on the Properties tool bar button.

To apply the default property settings to selected controls

To apply the default property settings to selected controls on the active form:

1 Select one or more controls in the Design view of the current form.

2 Choose Layout Apply Default.

You can display the default property settings for a control by choosing Properties from the View menu and then choosing the tool whose properties you want to examine from the toolbox.

To change default property settings for new controls

To create a new default from the property settings of selected controls on the current form:

1 Select a control on a form in Design view.

2 Choose Layout Change Default.

Changes to the default apply to the current form or report only.

After you set properties for controls, you can select several control types simultaneously, and then choose Change Default.

Headers and Footers

Headers and footers are composed of text or graphics and are displayed at the top or bottom of the section of the form to which they belong.

Two kinds of headers and footers are available for use on a form: page and form, described in the following:

- The *page header and footer* appear at the top and bottom of each page when printed. Page headers and footers do not appear in Form view.

- The *form header and footer* are printed before and after each form.

Headers and footers are always added to a form in pairs. If you do not want to display both, you can suppress the header or the footer from being printed by dragging the bottom edge up until the height has reached zero. You can only resize a header or footer to zero height if you have not placed any controls there.

Headers and footers are removed in pairs as well. When you remove a header and footer, any controls you placed on them are deleted.

To display or remove the form header and form footer sections

To toggle between the display or removal of a form header and form footer, choose **L**ayout Form **H**dr/Ftr. When a form header and/or footer is displayed, a check mark appears next to this menu item.

If you remove an existing form header and form footer section, any controls you placed on it are removed as well. These controls will not reappear if you redisplay the header or footer.

To display or delete the page header and page footer sections

To toggle between the display or deletion of the page header and footer that appear if the form is printed, choose **L**ayout **P**age Hdr/Ftr.

If you remove an existing form header and form footer section, any controls you placed on it are removed and will not reappear if you redisplay the header or footer.

Filters

You can specify criteria in a filter to create a temporary subset of a form's records, optionally sort the records, and display them in a form or form datasheet.

A filter cannot be saved as a filter. If you want to use a filter more than one time, you must save the filter as a query.

To define a new filter

To display the Form Filter window, in which you can define a new filter or revise an existing one:

1 Choose **R**ecords Edit **F**ilter/Sort. The Form Filter window appears.

2 If you want to use an existing query as a filter for the current form, select **F**ile **L**oad From Query in the Form Filter window.

3 Select a field by dragging a field name from the field list in the top part of the window to a column in the lower half. You can also select a field by selecting the field list at the top of each column and scrolling through the drop-down list for the names of available fields.

4 Select how you want the filtered data to be sorted by selecting a sort method from the Sort row: Ascending, Descending, or <not sorted>.

5 Enter any desired criteria in the criteria row.

6 Select **R**ecords App**l**y Filter/Sort to apply the filter you have created.

Shortcut: Click on the Edit Filter/Sort tool bar button.

To apply a filter

To apply a filter you created in the Filter window and display the resulting dynaset, choose **R**ecords Apply Filter/Sort.

You can apply a filter only to a form or its datasheet.

 Shortcut: Click on the Apply Filter/Sort tool bar button.

Saving Forms

After you design your form, you must save the form design in the database if you want to use it again.

To save a form

To save changes to the design of an existing form and replace the previous version of the form with the current version, choose **F**ile **S**ave.

To save a newly created form or make a copy of the current form with a new name

To save a newly created form or make a copy of the current form with a new name:

1 Select **F**ile Save **A**s. The Save As dialog box appears.

2 Enter a name for the form you are saving in the Name text box.

3 Click on the OK button to close the Save As dialog box and save the form.

Shortcut: Press F12.

To save any modifications to a form and its underlying datasheet

To save modifications to the layout of an existing form and its datasheet by replacing the previous version with the current version, choose **F**ile **S**ave Form.

The **S**ave Form command does not save data. Data is saved when you add or change records in a form or subform or when you choose the Save Rec**o**rd command.

> **Shortcut:** Press Shift+F12.

To save a form as a report

To save a form as a report:

To save a form as a report, choose **F**ile Save As Rep**o**rt.

Printing

When you need hard copy of your data, you may choose one of several ways to send your data to a printer. Print forms and reports to see attractive, formatted output. Print the Datasheet view of your data to get the maximum information on the least amount of paper.

You can print in form in Datasheet, Design, and Form views. Reports can be printed from Design view or Print Preview.

You can only print the Datasheet view of a table or query. The Print options are not available in Table Design view or Query Design view.

Access Basic modules can only be printed from Design view.

Macros cannot be printed.

To print the active form in Datasheet, Design, or Form view

To print the active form in Datasheet, Design, or Form view:

1 Choose File **P**rint. The Print dialog box appears.

2 To print the entire form, select the **A**ll option in the Print Range group.

or

To print a range of records you selected in the form, select the S**e**lection option in the Print Range Group.

or

To specify the pages you want to print, select **P**ages in the Print Range Group, and then enter the beginning page in the **F**rom text box and the ending page in the **T**o text box.

3 To specify the resolution of the print job, select an option from the Print **Q**uality list. The print quality options may differ, depending on your printer driver.

4 Select the Print to F**i**le check box if you want to send output to a file instead of a printer. You can select this option if you don't have a printer installed.

5 If you want more than one set of copies printed, enter a value in the **C**opies text box.

6 To collate printed copies of a document (arranged the pages in complete sets), select the Collate Copies check box.

7 To change printers and connections, select the **S**etup button.

8 To begin printing, click on the OK button.

When you print a form, you are really printing the whole dynaset of the form, not just the records displayed on-screen.

When you select the **P**rint command from Form view, your data is printed as it appears in Form view. From the

Datasheet view, the data is printed as a datasheet. Data is printed from Design view in the same layout as the data printed from Form view, but without any graphic elements.

To view a form on-screen as it will look after it is printed

To view a datasheet on screen as it will appear after it is printed, select File Print Preview from Design view, Datasheet view, or Form view.

 Shortcut: Click on the Print Preview tool bar button.

To select a printer

To select a printer and printer options for printing a query datasheet:

1 Select File Print Setup. The Print Setup dialog box appears.

2 Select the Default Printer option button if you want to use the default Windows printer. If you have more than one printer installed, you can select the Specific Printer option button and then select a printer from the Specific Printer list.

3 To print a form in *portrait style* (vertical paper orientation), select the Portrait option button in the Orientation group.

or

To print a form in *landscape style* (horizontal paper orientation), select the Landscape option button in the Orientation group.

4 Select a size from the Size list in the Paper group to specify the size of the paper you are printing on.

5 Specify the paper source for your printer by selecting a source from the Source list in the Paper group.

6 Select the Data Only option to separate data from graphic elements in a datasheet, form, or report,

and print only the data without any borders, graphics, or gridlines.

7 To change the margin settings, enter new values for the margins in the Left, Right, Top, and Bottom text boxes in the Margins group.

8 To specify the default settings for the printer you chose, select the Options button. The options available to you in the dialog box depend on your selected printer. Click on the OK button to return to the Print Setup dialog box.

9 The More button is available when you are printing a form or report.

When you select the More button, the Print Setup dialog box expands downward to reveal additional print options, covered in steps 10 through 17. These additional options are for forms and reports only.

10 Enter a new value in the Items Across text box to change the number of columns in the printout.

11 Enter a new value in the Row Spacing text box to change the default spacing between rows of printout.

12 Enter a new value in the Column Spacing text box to change the default spacing between columns of output printout.

13 Select the Same As Detail check box in the Item Size group to print out the entire form or report. If you unselect this check box, the print area is defined by the values displayed in the Width and Height text boxes.

14 Enter a value in the Width text box in the Item Size group if you want to change the width of the area to be printed.

15 Enter a value in the Height text box in the Item Size group if you want to change the height of the area to be printed.

16 Select the **H**orizontal option button in the Item Layout group if you want successive items printed in a horizontal layout from left to right.

17 Select the **V**ertical option button in the Item Layout group if you want successive items printed in a vertical layout, from top to bottom.

18 Click on the OK button to close the Print Setup dialog box.

Closing the Form Design Window

When you are finished working with a form, you can close its window to make more room for other windows on-screen.

To close the active Form

To close the Form Design window, the Form Datasheet window, or the Form View window without exiting Microsoft Access, make the window current and choose **F**ile **C**lose.

Reports

One of the most important reasons for storing data records is so that you can display the information to others. Often, you will want to organize and present your data in a format that is easier to read and understand than a datasheet.

Microsoft Access makes it easy for you to create attractive printed reports based on multiple tables or queries. ReportWizards are special tools provided with Microsoft Access that help you create reports by asking you to answer some basic questions about how you want to present your data and then doing all the layout work for you. The Report Design view enables you to start a report from scratch or customize a report that ReportWizard helped you design.

The Report menu replaces any other menu if you open or switch to a report window. You can open a report in Design view or in Preview.

Creating a Report

You have two options when you want to create a new report. You can go directly to Report Design view to start with a blank report, or you can choose to have the ReportWizard help you design a basic report.

To create a new report

To create a new report:

1 Choose **F**ile Ne**w R**eport. The New Report dialog box appears.

2 Enter the name of a table or query on which to base the new report, or select a name from the Select a **T**able/Query drop-down list.

3 Select the Report**W**izards button for step-by-step help in creating the report layout you want. If no tables or queries are in your database, the Report**W**izards button is disabled, or *grayed out*.

4 Select the **B**lank Report button to create a blank report and enter the Report Design view.

Shortcuts: Click on the New Report tool bar button.

Click on the Report object button in the Database window, and then click on the **N**ew button at the top of the Database window.

Using the ReportWizard

The ReportWizard takes most of the work out of designing a basic report. You just answer a few simple questions, and the Microsoft Access ReportWizard produces an attractive report based on your data.

Even if you are experienced at designing reports, the ReportWizard can speed development by quickly giving you a basic report you can customize, taking far less effort than starting from a blank report.

To use the ReportWizard to design a report:

1 Choose **F**ile Ne**w R**eport. The New Report dialog box appears.

2 Enter the name of a table or query on which to base the new report, or select a name from the Select a Table/Query drop-down list.

3 Select the Report**W**izard button. The Microsoft Access ReportWizard dialog box appears.

4 You can choose from three ReportWizards: Single-column, Group/Totals, and Mailing Label.

A Single-column report displays the fields from each data record in a single column, going down the page. Each value is on a separate line, with a descriptive label to its left.

A Group/Totals report separates your data into groups (based on grouping criteria you specify) and optionally sorts it, and displays records in a tabular format. Your report can display a total for each group, and a grand total for all the groups in your report.

A Mailing Label report displays the fields that you choose in one of many built-in mailing label formats.

Select which style of report you want and then follow the detailed directions in each dialog box that tell you how to proceed.

5 After you have specified the fields to be used in your report, Access asks you to select the look of the report. You may choose from Executive format, Presentation Format, or Ledger format. Select the option button next to each and look at the picture of the magnifying glass to see the differences in the look of these three formats. Select the **N**ext> button when you are through.

6 The Report Title defaults to the name of the table or query that you based it on. To give the report a different name, enter a report name in the Report Name: text box.

7 If you want Microsoft Access to arrange the display so that all of the fields in your report are visible on one page, select the Fit all fields on one page check box.

8 The ReportWizard is finished. Choose the Print Preview button to see how your new report will look when it is printed, or select the Design button to go to Report Design view, where you can customize your report.

Opening Reports

You can open an existing report in Design view, to modify its design and the layout of controls, or in Print Preview, to see a representation of how the report will appear after it has been printed.

To open an existing report

To open a report in Design view:

1 From the active Database window, choose **V**iew **R**eports, or click on the Report object button on the left side of the Database window with your mouse. A list of existing reports appears in the Database window.

2 Choose the **D**esign button at the top of the Database window.

To open a report in Print Preview:

1 From the active Database window, choose **V**iew **R**eports, or click on the Report object button on the left side of the Database window. A list of existing reports appears in the Database window.

2 Choose the **P**review button at the top of the Database window.

To display the list of reports in the database

To display a list of all the reports in the active database, choose **V**iew **R**eports.

REPORTS **145**

> **Shortcut:** Click on the Report object button in the Database window.

Sorting and Grouping

Microsoft Access enables you to separate your data into groups on a report, and sort the groups and data within the groups.

To specify how your report's data should be grouped and sorted

To toggle the display of the Sorting and Grouping box in a report's Design view:

1 Choose **V**iew **S**orting and Grouping. The Sorting and Grouping dialog box appears.

2 Select from the Field/Expression column a field name by which to sort your data, or enter an expression in one of the spaces in the column. You may select multiple fields by which to sort your report data.

3 For every field or expression you specify in the Field/Expression column, you can choose the sort order. Tab to the Sort Order column, or select the line to the right of the field you are setting the sort order for. Then open the list by pressing Alt+Down arrow or by clicking on the down-arrow button. Select Ascending or Descending for the sort order.

4 Select values for each field in the Group properties pane of the Sorting and Grouping dialog box.

A Group Header displays text or graphics at the top of a group in a report. To display a group header for the selected field, choose Yes in the Group Header drop-down list.

A Group Footer displays text or graphics at the bottom of a group in a report. To display a group footer for the selected field, choose Yes in the Group Footer drop-down list.

The Group On property determines how values will be grouped. Select an option from the Group On drop-down list. Options vary depending on the data type of the field you are grouping.

Group Interval specifies the interval in which values that are grouped together must fall.

5 To close the Sorting and Grouping box, press Alt+F4, choose **V**iew **S**orting and Grouping again from the menu, or click on the Sorting and Grouping tool bar button.

You can set the sorting and grouping criteria before or after you draw controls on the report.

When the Sorting and Grouping window is open, a check mark appears next to the **V**iew **S**orting menu item.

 Shortcut: Click on the Sorting and Grouping tool bar button.

Calculated Controls

A calculated control on a report is actually a text box control that contains an expression instead of a text string. The expression is assigned to the Control Source property of the control.

Microsoft Access evaluates the expression each time it is encountered, and displays a value that matches the results of the calculation of the expression. A calculated control can operate on data from one or more fields from the underlying table or query.

You can use a calculated control when you want Microsoft Access to generate a value for a field automatically.

To create a calculated control

To create a calculated control on a report in Design view:

1 Add a text box or other control to the form or report.

2 While the control is selected, click on it again.

3 Enter the expression that will determine what the control displays.

Microsoft Access doesn't store the result of a calculated field in a table but recomputes it each time the record is displayed.

Headers and Footers

You can use three kinds of headers and footers in a report. Headers and footers are composed of text or graphics and are displayed at the top or bottom of the section of the report.

The report header and footer are only printed once—at the start and end of the report. The page header and footer are printed once on each page. The group header and footer are printed before and after each group on the report.

Headers and footers are always added to the report in pairs. If you do not want to display both, you can suppress the header or the footer from being printed by using the mouse to drag the bottom edge up until the height has reached zero. You can only resize a header or footer to zero height if you have not placed any controls there.

Headers and footers are removed in pairs. When you remove a header and footer, any controls you had placed on them previously will be deleted.

Display or remove the report header or footer sections

To toggle between the display or removal of a report header and report footer for your report, choose **Layout** Report **H**dr/Ftr.

When a report header and/or footer is displayed, a check mark appears next to this menu item.

Display or remove the page header and page footer sections

To toggle between the display or deletion of the page header and footer that appear if the form is printed, choose **L**ayout **P**age Hdr/Ftr.

Display or remove the group header and group footer sections

A Group Header displays text or graphics at the top of a group in a report. To display a group header for the selected field, choose Yes in the Group Header drop-down list.

A Group Footer displays text or graphics at the bottom of a group in a report. To display a group footer for the selected field, choose Yes in the Group Footer drop-down list.

Printing

When you need hard copy of your data, you may choose one of several ways to send your data to a printer. Print forms and reports to see visually attractive, formatted output. Print the Datasheet view of your data to get the maximum information on the least amount of paper.

You can print in form in Datasheet, Design, and Form views. Reports can be printed from Design view or Print Preview.

You can only print the Datasheet view of a table or query. The Print options will not be available in Table Design view or Query Design view.

Access Basic modules can only be printed from Design view.

Macros cannot be printed.

To print the active report in Design view or Print Preview

To print the active report in Design view or Print Preview:

1 Choose **F**ile **P**rint. The Print dialog box appears.

2 To print the entire report, select the **A**ll option in the Print Range group.

or

To print a range of records you have selected in the report, select the S**e**lection option in the Print Range Group.

or

To specify the pages you want to print, select **P**ages in the Print Range Group, and then enter the beginning page in the **F**rom text box and the ending page in the **T**o text box.

3 To specify the resolution and speed of the print job, select an option from the Print **Q**uality list. The print quality options may differ, depending on your printer driver.

4 Select the Print to File check box if you want to send report output to a file instead of a printer. You can select this option if you don't have a printer installed.

5 To specify if more than one set of copies should be printed, enter a value in the **C**opies text box.

6 To collate printed copies of a document (arranged the pages in complete sets), select the Collate Cop**i**es check box.

7 To change printers and connections, select the **S**etup button. For more information on selecting a printer, see Chapter 5, "Working with Datasheets."

8 To begin printing, click on the OK button.

To view a form on-screen as it will look after it is printed

To view a datasheet on screen as it will appear after it is printed, choose File Print Preview from Design view, Datasheet view, or Form view.

 Shortcut: Click on the Print Preview tool bar button.

To toggle the Sample Preview display

To toggle the display of the Sample Preview window, which enables you to look quickly at the basic layout of your report, choose File Sample Preview.

Sample Preview can display only a limited number of records. It ignores criteria and joins in an underlying query. Choose File Print Preview if you want to view your report exactly as it will be printed.

When the Sample Preview window is open, a check mark appears next to this menu item.

To select a printer

To select a printer and printer options for printing a query datasheet:

1 Choose File Print Setup. The Print Setup dialog box appears.

2 Select the Default Printer option button if you want to use the default Windows printer. If you have more than one printer installed, you can select the Specific Printer option button, and select a printer from the Specific Printer list.

3 To print a report in portrait style (vertical paper orientation), select the Portrait option button in the Orientation group.

or

To print a report in landscape style (horizontal paper orientation), select the **L**andscape option button in the Orientation group.

4 Select a size from the Si**z**e list in the Paper group to specify the size of the paper on which you are printing.

5 Specify the paper source for your printer by selecting a source from the **S**ource list in the Paper group.

6 Select the Data Onl**y** option to separate data from graphic elements in a report, and print only the data without any borders, graphics, or gridlines.

7 To change the margin settings, enter new values for the margins in the **L**eft, Ri**g**ht, **T**op, and **B**ottom text boxes in the Margins group.

8 To specify the default settings for the printer you chose, select the **O**ptions button. The options available to you in the dialog box depend on your selected printer. Click on the OK button to return to the Print Setup dialog box.

9 The **M**ore button is available when you are printing a form or report. When you choose the **M**ore button, the Print Setup dialog box expands downward to reveal additional print options in steps 10 through 17. These additional options are for forms and reports only.

10 Enter a new value in the Items **A**cross text box to change the number of columns in the printout.

11 Enter a new value in the Ro**w** Spacing text box to change the default spacing between rows of printout.

12 Enter a new value in the Col**u**mn Spacing text box to change the default spacing between columns of output printout.

13 Select the S**a**me As Detail check box in the Item Size group to print out the entire form or report. If you unselect this check box, the print area is defined by the values displayed in the Width and Height text boxes.

14 Enter a value in the Width text box in the Item Size group if you want to change the width of the area to be printed.

15 Enter a value in the Height text box in the Item Size group if you want to change the height of the area to be printed.

16 Select the **H**orizontal option button in the Item Layout group if you want successive items printed in a horizontal layout from left to right.

17 Select the **V**ertical option button in the Item Layout group if you want successive items printed in a vertical layout, from top to bottom.

18 Click on the OK button to close the Print Setup dialog box.

Saving Reports

After you finish designing your report, you must save the design in the database so that you can use it again.

To save a new report or make a copy of the current report with a new name

To save the structure and design of a new report or create a copy of the active report and save the copy under a new name:

1 Choose **F**ile Save **A**s. The Save As dialog box appears.

2 Enter a name for the report you are saving in the Name text box.

3 Click on the OK button to close the dialog box.

> **Shortcut:** Press F12.

To save a report

To save changes to the design of an existing report and replace the previous version of the report with the current version, choose File **S**ave.

Changing Names

You can rename any database object when the Database window is active.

To rename a report

To rename a report;

1 Select the object you want to rename in the Database window.

2 Choose File Rena**m**e. The Rename dialog box appears with the original name of the report displayed in the title bar.

3 Enter a new name for the object in the **R**eport Name: text box, and click on the OK button.

If you change the name of a database object, you should find and update any references to that object that use the original name so that Microsoft Access can locate the object later.

Closing the Report Design Window

When you are finished working with a report, you can close its window to make more room for other windows on-screen.

To close the active Report Design window

To close the active Report Design window without exiting Microsoft Access, choose **F**ile **C**lose.

Macros

The Macro menu appears when you open or switch to a macro window. You can open a macro in Design view or run the macro from the Database window.

Macros add to the capabilities of your database. A macro is a sequence of built-in commands, or *actions* that you put together that Microsoft Access can carry out.

You can specify a macro name as the property of some controls on forms and reports. On certain events, such as the opening or closing of a form, or the editing of a control, the macro whose name is listed for that event is automatically executed by Microsoft Access. In this way, you can greatly extend the capabilities of your database.

Creating Macros

A macro instructs Microsoft Access to perform each action in the order that it is listed in the macro, operating on the database object or data you specify.

To create a new macro

To create a new macro in the current database:

1 To create a new macro in the current database, choose File New Macro. The Macro Window appears.

2 Select a cell in the Action column. Click on the down arrow, or press Alt+Down arrow to display the action list. Select the action you want from the drop-down list, or enter an action name in the Action column.

3 Enter a comment in the Comment column that describes the effect this action has.

4 After you select an action in the Action column, options for the arguments for the action appear in the lower pane of the window. These will differ depending on which of the 42 built-in actions you have chosen. Hint text will appear in the right half of the lower pane that describes what you need to enter in each text box. You can see the hint text for an option by placing the cursor in one of the text boxes.

5 Add as many actions as you need to. When you are finished, save the macro.

Microsoft Access carries out the actions in the order they are listed.

You can move from the top to the bottom of the Macro Design window by pressing F6, or using your mouse to click in the half of the window you want.

 Shortcut: Click on the Macro object button in the Database window, and then choose the New button.

Opening an Existing Macro

You can open a macro or macro group that has been saved, for the purpose of editing or examining the actions in it.

To list macros in the database

To display a list of all the macros in the active database, choose **View Macros**.

MACROS

 Shortcut: Click on the Macro object button in the Database window.

To open an existing macro
Open an existing macro by choosing **F**ile **N**ew **M**acro while the Database window is active.

 Shortcut: Click on the Macro object button on the left side of the Database window, and then click on the New button at the top of the Database window.

Running a Macro

In Microsoft Access, you can run a macro in several different ways:

- You can link a macro to certain events that occur in a form or report. When the event occurs, the macro runs automatically.

- You can link a macro to a command button on a data entry form that will execute when the button is selected.

- You can create your own customized menu bar and run a macro from a command on this menu bar.

- You can assign a macro to a key combination.

A special macro named Autoexec runs automatically every time you open the database, and the Run Macro action can run a macro from within another macro.

To run a specific macro in a macro group
To run a specific macro in a macro group:

1 Choose **F**ile **R**un Macro. The Run Macro dialog box appears.

2   Enter the macro group name, followed by a period and the macro name you want to run, in the Macro Name text box, or select a macro group name from the Macro Name drop-down list and add the period and macro name after the selection.

3   Click on the OK button to close the dialog box and run the macro.

To run a macro
To run a Microsoft Access macro:

1   Choose **File Ru**n Macro. The Run Macro dialog box appears.

2   Enter a macro name in the Macro **N**ame text box, or select a macro from the drop-down list.

3   Click on the OK button to close the dialog box and start the macro.

To run the macro from the Macro Design window, choose **M**acro **R**un.

If you have not saved your macro since making changes, Microsoft Access asks you to do so before you run the macro.

 Shortcut: Click on the Run Macro tool bar button.

To single-step through a macro
Single stepping enables you to run the actions in a macro one step at a time. To toggle single stepping on or off:

1   Choose **M**acro **S**ingle Step when a Macro Design view window is active.

2   Choose **M**acro **R**un. The Macro Single Step dialog box appears.

3   Choose the **S**tep button to run the action shown in the dialog box. The next action then appears in the dialog box (unless the first action causes an error).

Select **S**tep once for each step in the macro that you want Access to complete.

4 Choose the **H**alt button to halt the running of the macro.

or

Choose the **C**ontinue button to run the remainder of the macro. Choosing Continue will turn off single stepping.

If you have turned single stepping on, it remains on for all macros until you turn it off.

When **S**ingle Step is active, a check mark appears next to this menu item.

 Shortcut: Click on the Macro Single Step tool bar button.

Displaying Columns

You can change the way the Macro Design window is displayed. The display of the Condition column and the Macro Names column can be toggled on and off.

To toggle display of the Macro Condition column

To display or hide the Condition column in the Macro window, choose **M**acro **C**onditions.

Any expressions you enter in the Condition column remain in effect even if the column is hidden.

Display the Condition column if you want to set conditions that determine when to run specific actions or call another macro from within a macro.

When the Condition column display is enabled, a check mark appears next to the command on the menu.

To hide the Condition column, choose the **C**onditions command again.

Shortcut: Click on the Macro Conditions tool bar button.

To toggle display of the Macro Name column

To display or hide the Macro Name column in the Macro window, choose View **M**acro Names.

Display this column if you create a macro group containing two or more macros. Name each macro within the macro group, and enter the names in the Macro Name column.

Macro names remain in effect even if you remove the Macro Name column from view.

When the Macro Name column is displayed, a check mark appears next to this menu item.

To remove the Macro Name column, choose the **M**acro Names command again.

 Shortcut: Click on the Macro Names tool bar button.

Changing the Name

You can rename any database object when the Database window is active.

To change the name of a macro group

To change the name of a macro group:

1 Choose **F**ile Rena**m**e. The Rename dialog box appears with the original name of the macro group displayed in the title bar.

2 Enter a new name for the macro group in the Macro Name text box, and click on the OK button.

MACROS **161**

If you change the name of a macro, you should find and update any references to that macro that use the original name so that Microsoft Access can locate it.

Saving the Macro

After designing a macro you must save it if you want to use it again.

To save a macro
To save the design of a macro, choose File Save.

> **Shortcut:** Press Shift+F12.

To save a new macro or make a copy of an existing macro with a new name
To save a new macro group or to create a copy of the macro group and save the copy under a new name:

1 Choose File Save As. The Save As dialog box appears.

2 Enter a name for the macro group you are saving in the Macro Name text box.

3 Click on the OK button to close the dialog box.

> **Shortcut:** Press F12.

Closing the Macro Design Window

When you are finished working with the Macro Design window you can close it to make more room for other windows on-screen.

To close the Macro Design window
To close the active Macro Design window without exiting Microsoft Access, choose **File Close**.

10

Security

An important feature that Microsoft Access offers is system security. You can create accounts for users and groups of users. A secure system enables the System Administrator to specify whether individual users or groups can see or make changes to a database object. Authorized users and guests are forced to log on to Microsoft Access by entering a user name and password in the Logon dialog box.

User Accounts

The system administrator of a secure system can create user accounts and groups of user accounts. Permissions to read and write data can be assigned to groups and users, specifying what access they can have to database objects.

It is easier to run a secure system when users are assigned into groups, because permissions can be assigned to the group rather than to individual users.

To create a new user account

To create a new user account:

1 Choose **Security Users**. The Users dialog box appears.

2 Choose the **N**ew button in the Users dialog box. The New User/Group dialog box appears.

3 Enter the new user's name in the **N**ame text box of the New User/Group dialog box.

4 Enter a four-digit number in the **P**ersonal ID Number text box of the New User/Group dialog box.

5 Click on the OK button to create the user account and return to the Users dialog box, where you may clear the new user's password, and add the user to or remove the user from available groups.

6 Choose the **C**lose button to close the Users dialog box.

To modify a user account

To modify a user account:

1 Choose **S**ecurity **U**sers. The Users dialog box appears.

2 Select a user name from the **N**ame list in the User group.

3 Select the **C**lear Password button if you need to wipe out the password that is currently assigned to this account.

4 If you want to add this user to an existing group, select the group to which you want to add this user from the **A**vailable Groups list, and then select the Add button to add the user to that group.

5 To delete a user from a group, select the group from which you want to delete this user from the **M**ember Of list, and then select the **R**emove button to remove the user from that group.

6 Choose the **C**lose button to close the Users dialog box.

To delete a user account

To delete a user account:

1 Choose **S**ecurity **U**sers. The Users dialog box appears.

SECURITY **165**

2 Select a user name from the **Name** list in the User group.

3 Select the **Delete** button.

4 Choose the **Close** button to close the Users dialog box.

Modifying Passwords

If you are running a secure system, it is a good idea to change your password on a regular basis, in case someone discovers your password and can log in to the system with system administrator permissions.

To change your password

To change the password on a Microsoft Access user account:

1 Choose **S**ecurity **C**hange Password. The Change Password dialog box appears.

2 Enter your current password in the **O**ld Password text box. (Microsoft Access displays all the characters you type as asterisks to protect confidentiality.)

3 Enter a new password in the **N**ew Password text box. (A password can contain up to 14 characters in any case and combination. Microsoft Access displays all the characters you type as asterisks to protect confidentiality.)

4 Enter the new password in the **V**erify text box, exactly as you entered it in the **N**ew Password text box. (Microsoft Access displays all the characters you type as asterisks to protect confidentiality.)

5 Click on the OK button after you finish to set the password and close the dialog box.

To clear a user's password

To clear the password on a Microsoft Access user account:

1. Choose **S**ecurity **U**sers. The Users dialog box appears.

2. Select a user name from the **N**ame list in the user group.

3. Select the **C**lear Password button if you need to wipe out the password that is currently assigned to the selected user account.

4. Click on the **C**lose button to close the Users dialog box.

Groups

You can create groups of users for your secure system, and define a set of permissions for the group that will apply to all the user accounts that are members of that group.

To create a new group

To create a new Microsoft Access user group:

1. Choose **S**ecurity **G**roups. The Groups dialog box appears.

2. Choose the Ne**w** button to create a new group. The New User/Group dialog box appears.

3. Enter a new group name in the **N**ame text box of the New User/Group dialog box.

4. Enter a four-digit number in the **P**ersonal ID Number text box of the New User/Group dialog box.

5. Click on the OK button to return to the Groups dialog box.

6. Choose the **C**lose button to close the Groups dialog box.

To delete an existing group

To delete an existing Microsoft Access user group:

1. Choose **S**ecurity **G**roups. The Groups dialog box appears.

2 Select a group name from the **Name** drop-down list.

3 Choose the **D**elete button. Microsoft Access asks you to confirm the deletion.

4 Click on the OK button to proceed with the deletion; click on the Cancel button to abort.

5 Choose the **C**lose button to close the Groups dialog box.

Permissions

Permissions are a set of properties or attributes that describe what access (if any) a user or a group of users has to a database object.

When a new database is first created, all users have full permissions to view and modify the data and design of it. You can change this default by modifying the permissions.

To assign user and group permissions for a database

To assign user and group permissions for a database:

1 Choose **S**ecurity **P**ermissions. The Permissions dialog box appears.

2 Select an object type from the **T**ype list in the Object group.

3 Select the name of the object from the **N**ame list in the Object group. You can change a user's or a group's permissions to access this selected object.

4 To display the current set of permissions for users, select the **U**sers option button in the User/Group group.

or

To display the current set of permissions for groups, select the **G**roups option button in the User/Group group.

5 Select a user or group name from the Name list in the User/Group group.

6 To change permissions for the selected user or group for the selected database object, select the appropriate check boxes in the Permissions group as follows:

To change read definition rights for all objects, select the **R**ead Definitions check box.

To change modify definition rights for all objects, select the **M**odify Definitions check box.

To change execute rights for macros, select the E**x**ecute check box.

To change read data rights for tables and queries, select the Read **D**ata check box.

To change modify data rights for tables and queries, select the M**o**dify Data check box.

To grant or deny full permissions on this database object to the selected user or group, select the **F**ull Permissions check box.

7 To permanently change the permissions, select the **A**ssign button.

8 Choose the **C**lose button to close the Permissions dialog box after you finish viewing and modifying permissions.

Access Basic

In Microsoft Access, you can create and edit sophisticated databases and maintain them without knowing a programming language. Access Basic provides a programmer with additional abilities to automate and extend the functionality of a database.

Creating Access Basic Modules

The Module menu appears whenever you open or switch to a Module Design window. You can open a module in Design view only. The only way to run a function in a module to call it from a macro. For more information on macros, see Chapter 9, "Macros."

To create a new module in the current database

To create an Access Basic code module, select File New Module from any window. The Module Window appears.

 Shortcuts: Select the Module object button in the Database window, and then select the New button.

Opening an Existing Module

After creating an Access Basic code module and saving it, you may have a need to modify the code.

To display the list of existing modules in the database

To display a list of all the modules in the active database, select **View Modules**.

> **Shortcut:** Select the Module Object button in the Database window.

To open an existing module

To open an existing module in a database:

1 In the Database window, select **View Mod**u**les**. A list of modules in the database appears in the database window.

2 Select the name of the module you want to open, and then choose the **D**esign button.

3 Microsoft Access opens the module in the Module Design window.

> **Shortcut:** Select the Module Object button in the Database window, and then double-click on the name of the module that you want to open.

Importing Code

Sometimes in your module, you may want to use code that was created and saved in text format. Text format is not the way Access Basic code is stored, so text files must be loaded and converted.

To import code in text form from a file

To import into a module code that has been saved in text format:

1 Select **File Load Text**. The Load Text dialog box appears.

2 Enter the name of the file containing the code you want to load in the File **N**ame text box, or select a file name from the File **N**ame drop-down list.

3 Choose the **R**eplace button to replace the text in the active module with the code you are loading.

or

Choose the **M**erge button to insert the text you are loading into the code in the active module without deleting any code.

or

Choose the Ne**w** button to create a new module from the text from the selected file.

or

Choose the Cancel button to exit the Load Text dialog box without loading a file.

After you select any of the buttons, the Load File dialog box closes.

Saving Modules

After you finish adding or changing code in a module, you must save the module so that your modifications are not lost.

To save a module

To save changes to the design of an existing module and replace the previous version of the module with the current version, choose **File S**ave.

To save module code as a text file

To export code from the current module in a text file on your disk:

1 Select **F**ile Save **T**ext. The Save Text dialog box appears.

2 In the File **N**ame text box, enter the name of the file that will contain the code you want to save in text format, or select an existing file name from the File Name drop-down list.

3 Choose the OK button to save the text file and close the Save Text dialog box.

Setting and Clearing Breakpoints

Breakpoints are a handy debugging tool. You can place a breakpoint on a statement in a function or subroutine to halt the execution of your code. You can then examine the values of variables or step through your code line-by-line to trace the execution and watch for errors.

To toggle a breakpoint on or off

To set or remove a breakpoint from a procedure, select **R**un **T**oggle Breakpoint.

The line that contains a breakpoint appears in bold type until you remove the breakpoint.

 Shortcuts: Press F9.

Click on the Toggle Breakpoint tool bar button.

To clear all breakpoints

To remove all breakpoints from all of your modules, select **R**un Clear All Breakpoints.

Debugging

Debugging is a part of programming in any language, and Access Basic is no exception. The statements that make up Access Basic can be very powerful when used properly, but sometimes an error creeps into your code. Microsoft Access provides you with several commands to make debugging your programs a little easier.

There are two ways you can trace your code through its execution. You can *single-step* into the procedure that was called and proceed line by line within it; or you can *procedure-step* to execute each called procedure as if it were a single statement.

To single-step through module code one statement at a time

To single-step through a module's code, select **R**un **S**ingle Step.

Single stepping and procedure stepping are the same except when the current statement contains a call to a procedure. To step into the procedure that was called and proceed line by line within the procedure, use the **Si**ngle Step command.

> **Shortcuts:** Press F8.
>
> Click on the Single Step tool bar button.

To procedure-step through module code

To execute code, one statement at a time, treating a call to a Sub or Function procedure as one step, select **R**un **P**rocedure Step after your program has been halted by a breakpoint.

Single-step and procedure-step are the same, except when the current statement contains a call to a procedure.

> **Shortcuts:** Press Shift+F8.
>
> Click on the Procedure Step tool bar button.

To resume execution of module code

To resume the execution of module code after a halt, select **R**un **C**ontinue.

Selecting the Continue command continues execution following the last statement that was executed before the halt. Selecting this command does not restart code execution unless the halt was caused by an error.

> **Shortcuts:** Press F5.
>
> Click on the Continue tool bar button.

To set the next statement to be executed in a module

To change the order in which your code executes so that the statement in which you placed the insertion point is the next statement to be executed, select **R**un Set **N**ext Statement.

To display the next executable statement

To show the next statement to be executed in a module, select **R**un S**h**ow Next Statement.

To display or hide the Immediate window

To toggle the display of the Immediate window, which you can use for testing and debugging code, select **V**iew Immediate Window.

To close the window, choose the Immediate Window command again. When the Immediate window is open, Microsoft Access displays a check mark next to the command.

To reinitialize code

To halt execution of Access Basic procedures and clear and reset all variables, select **R**un **R**einitialize. After this command you cannot continue execution.

> **Shortcut:** Click on the Reinitialize tool bar button.

To compile all procedures

Every time you add code or modify code, you must recompile it before Microsoft Access can run it.

To compile all of the procedures in all the modules in the current database, select **R**un Compile **A**ll.

If you run an uncompiled Function or Sub procedure, Microsoft Access automatically compiles the procedure.

To specify command-line arguments

Access Basic accepts command-line arguments. This means that you can specify switches and other information at the same time that you issue the command to run the program. The Command$ function retrieves any command-line arguments so that your program can use them.

You can use this command to debug code that uses the Command$ function.

To test your code's response to various command-line arguments:

1 Select **R**un **M**odify Command$. The Modify Command$ dialog box appears.

2 Enter in the String Returned by Command$ Function text box the new command-line argument you want your code to test.

3 Click on the OK button to close the Modify Command$ dialog box.

Displaying Modules and Procedures

Several commands help you customize the display in the Module Design window. You can display the next or previous procedure, move through the available procedures in order, or select a procedure to display from a list.

You can split the window displaying a procedure in two parts. By doing this, you can keep two sections of the same procedure on-screen at the same time.

To display the next procedure
To display the next procedure in the current module, select **View Next Procedure**.

> **Shortcuts:** Press Ctrl+Down arrow.
>
> Click on the Next Procedure tool bar button.

To display the previous procedure
To display the previous procedure in the current module, select **View Previous Procedure**.

> **Shortcuts:** Press Ctrl+Up arrow.
>
> Click on the Previous Procedure tool bar button.

View all modules and related procedures
To list all the modules and their procedures so that you can use the command to move to a specific procedure within any module in the database:

1 Select **View Procedures**. The View Procedures dialog box appears.

2 From the **M**odules list, select the module whose code you want to see.

3 From the **P**rocedures list, select the procedure that you want to display from the selected module.

4 Click on the OK button to view the selected module procedure.

> **Shortcut:** Press F2.

To split the Module window

To split the Module window so that you can view two procedures at the same time, select **V**iew Split **W**indow.

When the Module window is split into two panes, Microsoft Access displays a check mark next to the command.

To return the window to single display, choose the Split **W**indow command again or drag the split bar back to just below the title bar.

Press F6 to move between the two panes.

Index

A

Access Basic, 169
   code modules, 169-170
      debugging, 173-176
      displaying, 176-177
      importing in text
         format, 170-171
      opening, 170
      saving, 171-172
      setting and clearing
         breakpoints,
         172-173
accessing databases, 34
adding
   records, 63-64
   rows, 98-99
   tables, 99-100
aligning controls, 128-130
Append queries, 102-104
appending records, 68-69
attaching tables from external
   databases to Microsoft
   Access, 49-50
Avg calculation type, 95

B-C

breakpoints, 172-173

calculated controls, reports,
   146-147
calculated fields, 94-97
calculations,
   summary, 95-98
   types, 95-96
cascading windows, 11
changes, saving, 114
Clipboard, *see* Windows
   Clipboard
closing
   databases, 38-39, 48
   datasheets, 81
   windows
      Form Datasheet, 140
      Form Design, 140
      Form View, 140
      Macro Design,
         161-162
      Query Design, 91-92
      Report Design, 153
code modules, 169-170
   debugging, 173-176
   displaying, 176-177
   importing in text format,
      170-171
   opening, 170
   printing, 84-85, 149
   saving, 171-172
   setting and clearing
      breakpoints, 172-173
columns
   frozen, 79-80
   hidden, 78-79
   Macro Design window,
      159-160
   width, 78
command buttons, 9
commands, grayed out, 12
compacting databases, 35
context-sensitive Help, 9-10
controls, 127
   aligning, 128-130
   calculated in reports,
      146-147
   hidden, 130
   sizing, 131
   tab order, 127-128
copying tables, 44-45
Count summary calculation
   type, 96
criteria, queries, 92
Crosstab queries, 104-106
Cue Cards, 10-11
customizing Microsoft Access,
   12-26

D

data
   exporting from Microsoft
      Access format to
      another, 55-59
   importing from other
      formats, 50-55
   reports, sorting and
      grouping, 145-146
   tables, 33
data entry forms, *see* forms
database objects, 33
   names, 35-36, 91
Database window, 9, 42
   macros, 155
databases, 33
   accessing, 34

attaching tables from
    external databases to
    Microsoft Access, 49-50
  closing, 38-39, 48
  compacting, 35
  creating, 33-34
  decrypting, 37-38
  encrypting, 36-37
  importing Microsoft, 50-51
  importing data from other
    formats, 50-55
  modifying, 35-36
  opening, 34-35
  repairing, 38
  Select Query, 87-88
  tables, 41
Datasheet options, 20-21
Datasheet view, 62-68
  forms, 123-124
    printing, 136
  keyboard shortcuts, 28-30
  queries, saving, 90-91
datasheets, 61-62
  closing, 81
  columns
    frozen, 79-80
    hidden, 78-79
    width, 78
  fonts, 80-81
  gridlines, 81
  objects
    embedding, 70-72
    linking, 72-73
  printing, 84-85
    query, 115-117
  records
    adding, 63-64
    appending, 68-69
    deleting, 67-68
    moving between,
      64-65
    multiuser
      environment, 65-66
    networks, 65-66
    saving, 74
    searching for, 74-77
    selecting, 73-74
    viewing, 62-63
  rows, height, 77-78, 81-82
debugging code modules,
  173-176
decrypting databases, 37-38
Delete queries, 106-107
deleting
  field rows, 43
  rows, 98-99
  tables, 99-100

delimited text
  exporting tables to, 56-57
  importing, 51-53
Design view, 82
  forms, 122-125
  keyboard shortcuts, 28
  macros, 155
  printing
    forms, 136
    modules, 149
    reports, 148-152
  queries, saving, 89-90
  reports, 144
display, 113-114
  code modules, 176-177
  data and field names,
    80-81
  tables, lists, 42
  windows
    hidden, 11
    Module Design,
      176-177
dynasets, 87-88
  summary calculations,
    97-98

E

embedding objects, 70-72
encrypting databases, 36-37
environment preferences, 12
environments, multiuser, data
  entry, 65
equi-joins, 101
exiting Microsoft Access, 39
exporting
  data from Access
    databases, 55-59
  table, 56-57
  text files, specifications,
    57, 59
expressions, 94-97

F

field names, fonts, 80-81
field rows
  deleting, 43
  inserting, 42-43
fields, 41
  calculated, 94-97
  creating, 42-43
  objects
    embedding, 70-72
    linking, 72-73
  selecting, 43

INDEX

files, importing spreadsheet, 54-55
filters, 134-135
First summary calculation type, 96
fixed width text
    exporting tables to, 56-57
    importing, 53-54
fonts, 80-81
footers, 133-134, 147-148
Form & Report Design options, 18-20
Form Datasheet window, closing, 140
Form Design window, closing, 140
Form view
    forms, 122-123
        printing, 136
    keyboard shortcuts, 28-30
    window, closing, 140
formats, data, importing, 50-55
forms, 61, 119-120
    controls, 127-131
    deleting records or rows, 67-68
    filters, 134-135
    FormWizards, 120-122
    grids, 130-131
    headers and footers, 133-134
    opening, 122
    printing, 84-85, 136-140
    properties, 132-133
    saving, 135-136
    views
        Datasheet, 123-124
        Design, 122-125
        Form, 122-123
FormWizard, 18, 120-122
frozen columns, 79-80

G

General options, 13-15
global keys, keyboard shortcuts, 26-27
graphs, 121
grayed out commands, 12
gridlines, 81
    forms, 130-131
grouping data for reports, 145-146

H-J

headers
    forms, 133-134
    reports, 147-148
height of rows, 77-78
Help menu, 9-10
hidden
    columns, 78-79
    windows, displaying, 11

importing
    code modules in text format, 170-171
    data from other formats, 50-55
    databases, Microsoft Access, 50-51
    files, spreadsheet, 54-55
    text
        delimited, 51-53
        files, specifications, 57, 59
        fixed width, 53-54
indexes, keys, 43-44
inserting field rows, 42-43
installing Microsoft Access, 5-6

joins, 100-101
    equi-joins, 101
    outer joins, 101-102
    self-join, 101

K-L

keyboard shortcuts
    Datasheet view, 28-30
    Design view, 28
    Form view, 28-30
    global keys, 26-27
    Module window, 30-31
Keyboard options, 16-17
keys, 43-44

Last summary calculation type, 96
layouts, datasheets, 81-82
linking objects, 72-73
list of table, displaying, 42
listing queries, 114-115

M

Macro Design options, 23
Macro Design window, 156
    closing, 161-162

columns, 159-160
macros, 155
  creating, 155-156
  groups, renaming, 160-161
  opening, 156-157
  running, 157-159
  saving, 161
Main/Subform, 121
Make Table queries, 107-108
Max summary calculation type, 95
menu bars, 8
Microsoft Access
  customizing, 12-26
  databases
    exporting data, 55-59
    importing, 50-51
  exiting, 39
  group, 6
  installing, 5-6
  screen, 7-9
  starting, 6-7
Min summary calculation type, 95
minimized icons, 11
modifying databases, 35-36
Module Design options, 23-24
Module Design window, 169-170
  display, 176-177
  keyboard shortcuts, 30-31
modules, *see* code modules
moving between records in datasheet, 64-65
multiuser environment, data entry, 65-66
multiuser options, 24-26

N-O

names of objects, database, 35-36
networks, records, 65-66

Object buttons, 9
objects
  database, 33, 91
  embedding, 70-72
  linking, 72-73
  see also database objects
OLE objects, 69-71
opening
  code modules, 170
  databases, 34-35
  forms, 122
  macros, 156-157
  tables, 42
operators, 92-94

options
  Datasheet, 20-21
  Form & Report Design, 18-20
  General, 13-15
  Keyboard, 16-17
  Macro Design, 23
  Module Design, 23-24
  multiuser, 24-26
  printers, 82-84
  printing, 17-18
  Query Design, 22
outer joins, 101-102

P

Palette window, 125-126
Parameter Query, 109-110
passwords, 165-166
permissions, 167-168
primary keys, 44
Print Preview, reports, 144-145
  printing, 148-152
printers, options, 82-84
printing
  datasheets, 84-85, 115-117
  forms, 136-140
  modules, 149
  options, 17-18
  reports, 136-140
    Design view, 148-152
    Print Preview, 148-152
procedure-stepping through code, 173
Program Manager groups, Microsoft Access, 6
programming languages, Access Basic, 169
properties, 46-47, 110-113, 132-133

Q

QBE (Query by Example), 5, 87
  rows, adding or deleting, 98-99
  summary calculation, 97
  tables, adding or deleting, 99-100
queries, 62, 87
  Append, 102-104
  criteria, 92
  Crosstab, 104-106
  datasheets, printing, 115-117
  Delete, 106-107

INDEX 183

deleting records or rows, 67-68
fields, calculated, 94-97
listing, 114-115
Make Table, 107-108
operators, 92-94
Parameter, 109-110
properties, 110-113
running, 88-89
saving
  in Datasheet view, 90-91
  in Design view, 89-90
Update Table, 108-109
Query by Example, *see* QBE
Query Design options, 22
Query Design view, 87
Query Design window, closing, 91-92

R

RDBMS (relational database management system), 5
records, 41-42, 62
  datasheet
    adding, 63-64
    appending, 68-69
    deleting, 67-68
    moving between, 64-65
    multiuser environment, 65-66
    networks, 65-66
    viewing, 62-63
  saving, 74
  searching databases for, 74-77
  selecting, 73-74
relational database management system (RDBMS), 5
relationships, tables, 47-48
repairing databases, 38
Report Design
  view, 141-142
  window, closing, 153
reports, 141
  calculated controls, 146-147
  data, sorting and grouping, 145-146
  Design view, 144
  headers and footers, 147-148
  Print Preview, 144-145
  printing, 84-85
    Design view, 148-152

Print Preview, 148-152
Report Design view, 141-142
ReportWizard, 141-144
saving, 152-153
ReportWizard, 19, 141-144
rows
  adding or deleting, 98-99
  deleting from tables, queries, or forms, 67-68
  height, 77-78
rulers, 126
running macros, 157-159

S

saving
  changes, 114
  code modules, 171-172
  datasheets, 81-82
  forms, 135-136
  macros, 161
  queries
    in Datasheet view, 90-91
    in Design view, 89-90
  records, 74
  reports, 152-153
  tables, 44
screens
  global keyboard shortcuts, 26-27
  Microsoft Access, 7-9
scroll bars, 8
Search dialog box, 10
searching datasheets for records, 74-77
security, users
  accounts, 163-165
  groups, 166-167
  passwords, 165-166
  permissions, 167-168
Select Query, 87-88
selecting
  fields, 43
  records, 73-74
self-joins, 101
shortcuts, *see* keyboard shortcuts
Single-column form, 121
single-stepping through code, 173
sizing controls, 131
sorting data for reports, 145-146
speadsheet files, importing, 54-55

specifications, text files, importing and exporting, 57-59
splitting Module Design window, 177
SQL (Structured Query Language) statements, 113
starting Microsoft Access, 6-7
statements, SQL (Structured Query Language), 113
Status bar, 9
subforms, 125
summary calculation, 95-98
    types, 95-96
switching
    views, 45-46
    windows, 12
system security, users accounts, 163-165
    groups, 166-167
    passwords, 165-166
    permissions, 167-168

T

tab order of controls, 127-128
Table Design view, 45-46, 82
Table Window Design view, 41
tables, 41
    adding or deleting, 99-100
    attaching from external databases to Microsoft Access, 49-50
    copying, 44-45
    creating, 41-42
    deleting records or rows, 67-68
    displaying list, 42
    exporting
        to delimited text, 56-57
        to fixed width text, 56-57
    opening, 42
    properties, 46-47
    relationships, 47-48
    saving, 44
Tabular form, 121
text
    delimited, exporting tables to, 56-57
    file specifications
        exporting, 57-59
        importing, 57-59
    fixed width, exporting tables to, 56-57
    format, importing code modules, 170-171
    importing
        delimited, 51-53
        fixed width, 53-54
tiling windows, 11
title bars, 7
tool bar, 8
toolbox, 126-127
tools
    ReportWizard, 141-144

U-V

Update Table queries, 108-109
User accounts, 163-165

Var summary calculation type, 96
viewing records, datasheet, 62-63
views
    Datasheet, 62-63, 67-68, 90-91
    Design, 82, 89-90
    Query Design, 87
    switching, 45-46
    Table Design, 45-46, 82

W-Z

Welcome to Microsoft Access dialog box, 7
width of columns, 78
Window list, 11
Windows Clipboard, 66-67
windows, 11
    cascading, 11
    Database, 9
    displaying hidden, 11
    hiding, 11
    icons minimized, 11
    Palette, 125-126
    Query Design, closing, 91-92
    switching, 12
    tiling, 11